The Waiter and Waitress Training Manual

The Waiter and Waitress Training Manual

Fourth Edition

Sondra J. Dahmer
and
Kurt W. Kahl

VNR VAN NOSTRAND REINHOLD
I(T)P ™ A Division of International Thomson Publishing Inc.

New York • Albany • Bonn • Boston • Detroit • London • Madrid • Melborne
Mexico City • Paris • San Francisco • Singapore • Tokyo • Toronto

I(T)P ™ A division of International Thomson Publishing, Inc.
The ITP logo is a trademark under license

Printed in the United States of America

For more information contact:

Van Nostrand Reinhold
115 Fifth Avenue
New York, NY 10003

Chapman & Hall GmbH
Pappelallee 3
69469 Weinheim
Germany

Chapman & Hall
2-6 Boundary Row
London
SE1 8HN
United Kingdom

International Thomson Publishing Asia
221 Henderson Road #05-10
Henderson Building
Singapore 0315

Thomas Nelson Australia
102 Dodds Street
South Melborne, 3205
Victoria, Australia

International Thomson Publishing Japan
Hirakawacho Kyowa Building, 3F
2-2-1 Hirakawacho
Chiyoda-ku, 102 Tokyo
Japan

Nelson Canada
1120 Birchmount Road
Scarborough, Ontario
Canada M1K 5G4

International Thomson Editores
Campos Eliseos 385, Piso 7
Col. Polanco
11560 Mexico D. F. Mexico

1 2 3 4 5 6 7 8 9 10 EDW—LT 01 00 99 98 97 96

Library of Congress Cataloging-in-Publication Data

ISBN 0-442-02110-0

CONTENTS

CONTENTS

PREFACE

Today it is necessary for waiters and waitresses to be well-trained in the technical skills of serving the customer, not only for job satisfaction and mastery but for the success of the restaurant where they work. This restaurant, in turn, must compete with other restaurants for the patronage of customers in the marketplace. As the market becomes more crowded and competition more intense, restaurants keep their competitive edge by having fresh wholesome food, unique menu items, attractive prices, interesting decor and settings, and, above all, superior service from well-trained waiters and waitresses.

Current research shows that service is one of the most important factors for the success of any restaurant One study concludes that service is about as important as food, and suggests that consumers are willing to travel extra distances to patronize full-service restaurants if excellent food and service are offered at a reasonable price. Another survey shows that restaurateurs believe, overwhelmingly, that the most important attribute for restaurants is to have friendly waiters and waitresses. Good and pleasant service leaves a lasting impression on those who are busy or tired and go out to relax and enjoy themselves.

Today people eat out to entertain business associates or for convenience due to hectic schedules or long commutes. Eating out in restaurants is also a time to relax, unwind, and be pampered. Fine dining may be an end in itself—treat, a form of entertainment, a means to celebrate a special occasion, or a chance to be served foods that might not be prepared at home None of these reasons for eating out can be enjoyed if the service is poor

To grow and flourish m the fast-paced decade of the 1990s and to distinguish themselves in the service area, restaurants are using formal waiter and waitress training to more effectively develop efficient, courteous servers with superior serving skills. *The Waiter and Waitresses Training Manual* is a great training tool that can help with this monumental task This book will help servers learn the knowledge and techniques of serving that will have an impact on their job performance, on their personal success, and ultimately, on the success of the restaurants themselves.

THE PURPOSE OF THIS BOOK

The fourth edition of the *Waiter and Waitress Training Manual* retains its design as a practical guide for those who want to learn how to serve food properly in a restaurant. Actual and prospective waiters and waitresses, as well as managers, supervisors, and teachers who train servers will find this an invaluable source for self-training or classroom use.

This new edition addresses "hot topics" in the restaurant industry that have not been covered in previous editions. Some of the current topics are accepting diversity of coworkers and patrons, preventing harassment, and keeping drugs out of the workplace. A new chapter, Chapter 6, covers safety and sanitation issues which, today, are as important as serving techniques. This new chapter also includes a discussion on handling emergencies like fires, tornadoes, electrical blackouts, and injured or ill guests.

Many sections from the previous edition have been updated or expanded. Among the many changes are those that discuss the qualifications for the job, teamwork by the staff, food allergies and preferences of guests, and trends in foods on the menu. There is new coverage on smoking in restaurants, serving the meal, suggestive selling techniques, a special amenities, and tipping. Chapter 7 includes a discussion of seating management software and the new touch-screen computers, and Chapter 8 incorporates a discussion of blush wines and "virgin" drinks.

Many other features make this edition exciting. There are new photographs, illustrations, and tables throughout the book. Four case problems, as well as an expanded glossary of restaurant terms, supplement the text.

The authors have retained and used words found in the dictionary based on standard use but are aware that there is a trend emerging toward alternative words that treat all jobs respectfully and are not gender-linked when gender is irrelevant. Words like waitress, bus boy and hostess may eventually be outmoded to be replaced by "serve," "waitperson," or "waitstaff" for waiter or waitress, "busser" instead of busboy or busgirl, and "host" in place of both host and hostess. We will appraise this trend for the next edition.

■ SUGGESTIONS TO TEACHERS AND TRAINERS

Use this manual as a textbook in a classroom or for training waiters and waitresses in a restaurant. Assign chapters, questions, and relevant projects

from the text, and build competencies through group discussion and practice. The questions at the end of the chapters and the cases and quiz at the
end of the book may be used to evaluate the trainee's knowledge of serving
procedures.

■ SUGGESTIONS TO THE WAITER, WAITRESS, OR TRAINEE

Use this manual as a self-training aid for learning how to serve or for
increasing your serving knowledge and skills. Abler reading the chapters,
answer the questions, complete as many of the projects as possible, and take
the quiz to review proper serving procedures.

A SPECIAL THANK YOU

We would like to acknowledge the help of Jerald C. Chesser, Ed. D., CEC, CCE, Mary Kay Linari, Paul-Michael Klein, Douglas C. Lance Jr., CHA, and John A. Balmores for their careful review of the third edition and suggestions for updating the book. Among the many other people who helped us with this latest edition, we would like to single out and thank Scott Koerner, Jane Bennett, R.D., Bernice Kelly, R.D., Frank Koszegi, Sandy Lien, Steve Heiring, Linda Krejci, Steve Gill, Maria Anna Kahl, Joe Dahmer, and Nate Dahmer who assisted us with questions or technical help. Thank you, also, to Elyse Rieder, photo researcher, who worked tirelessly on updating our photography, to Amy Shipper, Editorial Assistant, for her hours of work with revision, and to the VNR production staff for artwork and fine-tuning the final manuscript. We are particularly grateful to our editor, Mimi Melek, who gave us excellent advice about how to revise our book to include current "hot topics" that would be of interest to our readers, answers to our questions about details, and endless help and support.

*The Waiter
and Waitress
Training
Manual*

1

THE WAITER
AND WAITRESS

The waiter and waitress, also referred to as servers, are restaurant employees who wait on the guests by making them feel welcome and comfortable, taking their orders, serving the meal, clearing the area, and setting the table for the next party of guests. The server also maintains the service areas of the dining room and kitchen so that everything is ready for smooth, efficient service. Chapter 1 discusses the advantages of a waiter's or waitress's job, the qualifications necessary to become a server, the personal appearance of the server on the job, the server's position in the organizational structure of the restaurant, and how the server functions as part of a team with fellow employees and supervisors.

While the server's tasks may seem obvious, many involve issues of greater concern to the customer and establishment as well as the server. These issues include accepting cultural diversity of coworkers and guests, freedom from harassment on the job, prevention of violence, and restaurant safety and sanitation. Although mentioned in Chapter 1, some of these issues are discussed in greater detail in future chapters.

ADVANTAGES OF THE POSITION

There are many advantages to holding a job as a waiter or waitress. These include monetary benefits, contact with people, minimal investment in wardrobe, pleasant surroundings, and job satisfaction. The following is a discussion of these advantages.

One of the advantages of being a waiter or waitress is that you may be compensated well for rendering services to guests in a restaurant. In some elegant restaurants, a waiter or waitress who gives good service can make more money in tips and wages than a cook, secretary, police officer, flight attendant, or school teacher. You may also be allowed free or reduced-priced meals from the restaurant.

Another advantage of being a waiter or waitress is that you are serving the public and can meet many interesting people. You may make new friends among people of all ages and from all walks of life. Occasionally you may be able to serve a celebrity.

A waiter or waitress needs only a minimal investment in clothes for work. Whereas a job in an office requires a large investment in business clothing, a waiter's or waitress's job requires only a few uniforms and comfortable shoes.

Some people find working in pleasant surroundings advantageous. Many restaurants have very elaborate decor and atmosphere. You may also have the opportunity to sample a variety of food.

Finally, you can gain personal satisfaction from doing a job exceptionally well. Compliments and tips from the guests and words of praise from your manager are your rewards for providing good service. Take pride in your job. Waiting tables can be a rewarding part-time position or full-time career providing you with a very good living. The skills and knowledge that you learn will translate to all aspects of your life.

QUALIFICATIONS FOR THE JOB

Management looks for employees who are reliable, cooperative, personable, healthy, clean and neat, knowledgeable, persuasive, and attentive, because they make good servers. To qualify for a position as a waiter or waitress, you must be:

1. **Reliable**. Management must be able to depend on you to fulfill the responsibilities for which you were hired. You must report to work on time, serve the customers properly, and complete all tasks assigned to you.

2. **Cooperative**. You must have a good attitude. You must be willing to work hard with coworkers in a common effort toward completing work assigned. Be a good team player, and if the team is successful you will be successful at your job. Being cooperative also means adapting to the policies of management. Be willing to work hard and learn. Keep focused on your job even under pressure and time restraints.

3. **Personable**. A waiter or waitress is chosen for his or her pleasant personality. Take the initiative to be friendly, patient, and courteous to guests, coworkers, and management, and never be rude. A server should have a good sense of humor. However, never be "familiar" with customers or use terms such as "folks," "honey," or "you guys" when addressing guests.

4. **Healthy**. Because a serving job requires the server to be in close contact with guests, coworkers, and food, you must be healthy. Staying healthy helps you avoid spreading disease and maintain a good appearance. A healthy server looks good, performs well on the job, and is able to lift and carry heavy trays.

5. **Clean and neat**. A server may be one of the only restaurant employees that the guest sees and must present a tidy appearance that reflects the image of a clean and neat restaurant. Particular attention should be made to hair, nails, and uniform.

6. **Knowledgeable**. A good waiter or waitress must learn appropriate serving methods and how to apply them in a smooth, efficient manner. You must know how to manage your time well. You must have an extensive knowledge of the food items on the menu. A working knowledge of basic math and simple computer skills are necessary to complete the guest's order and total the check properly. Experience is desirable but technical knowledge can be learned.

7. **Persuasive**. You must have the ability to sell yourself, the restaurant, and menu items during the course of service to the customer. To do this you must be able to communicate well. Your persuasive talents ensure that the customer's wants and needs are met, and suggestive selling increases the size of the check, restaurant profits, and, in the end, your tip.

8. **Attentive**. Guests may need their waiter or waitress at any time during the meal, so a good server always concentrates on the job and never leaves a station unattended. You must be aware of the progress of the meal at each table and anticipate needs as they arise. Be aware of emptied water glasses and coffee cups, but not to an excessive degree. Take pride in the appearance of the dining room by keeping it orderly as you work.

▐ PERSONAL APPEARANCE ON THE JOB

Your appearance on the job influences the first impression and, consequently, the lasting impressions that a customer has of the restaurant. Because you are one of the few members of the restaurant staff a guest sees, a customer may judge the restaurant largely by your appearance and service.

Figure 1-1 You are the main restaurant employee the customer sees, so be sure your uniform is clean and neat. Your appearance can help create a good impression for the entire operation.

THE UNIFORM

A uniform is a garment that identifies the occupation of the wearer. Nurses, police officers, sailors, and pilots, as well as waiters and waitresses, wear uniforms. The appearance of your uniform leaves an impression on your guests (Figure 1–1). If it is clean and neat, you project a sanitary image of the restaurant. If your uniform is soiled or wrinkled, you will not impress the guests favorably, and the guests, deciding that your uniform reflects the standards of the whole operation, may never return.

The uniform should fit well; if it is too tight, it restricts your movement. A waitress's skirt should have a fashionable hem length, but not be so short that she feels conspicuous when reaching or bending. A waitress's pants should fit smoothly and not be too tight or restrictive. Waiters must be sure that their slacks are properly pressed and that their jackets and ties are clean and neat.

The server should wear a clean uniform each work day and keep an extra one at work in case of emergency. Skirts, pants, jackets, and ties should be neat, clean, and pressed. Most uniforms today are made of synthetic fiber blends that are easy to maintain. If you do spill food on a uniform, remove the stains as soon as possible and launder according to manufacturer's directions. Uniforms in disrepair are as unattractive as soiled uniforms. Repair torn hems and seams, and replace buttons before you wear the uniform again.

The uniform should fit well; if it is too small, it restricts movement. Pants should fit smoothly and not be too tight. A waitress's skirt should have a fashionable hem length, but not so short that she feels conspicuous when reaching or bending.

Shoes are part of the uniform and should have attention daily. Buy sturdy waiter's or waitress's shoes with closed toes, low heels, and arch supports (see Figure 1–1). Shoes should have rubber soles to minimize slips and falls. Have worn heels and soles repaired and be sure your shoes are clean and polished for work. Have a second pair of shoes at work, especially if you are a full-time waiter or waitress, and change your shoes occasionally to prevent feet and back problems.

Waitresses might consider support hose for comfort and panty hose for good appearance in a job that requires reaching and bending. Keep an extra pair in your locker or purse in case of a run.

Wedding and engagement rings and classic watches may be worn, but decorative jewelry such as bracelets, dinner rings, and lapel pins are not appropriate as part of a uniform. Decorative jewelry does not look professional and is not sanitary when you are working with food.

GROOMING

Careful attention must be given to your personal hygiene and grooming because you are working with the public. In order to look well physically, you must have the proper amount of rest each night. Bathe daily and wear an antiperspirant to prevent body odors. Brush your teeth, use a mouthwash, and see a dentist twice a year. Use breath mints or breath sprays at work. Never smoke or chew gum in front of guests.

Wear your hair in a simple, stylish manner pulled back from your face, and avoid extreme coiffures. Be sure it is clean and combed. Use effective hair restraints to prevent the contamination of food or food-contact surfaces. Invisible hairnets that do not detract from your appearance are available today, as well as caps, headbands, barrettes, and other restraints designed to be part of the uniform.

Waiters and waitresses should be sure their hands and nails are clean because they are on display. Scrub your nails and trim them to a short, even length. Waitresses may wear a conservative color or clear nail polish.

Waiters must be cleanshaven, and waitresses should use a minimum of make-up, such as a conservative application of eye make-up and lipstick. Perfumes and colognes do not enhance food aromas and should not be worn.

Keep your hands away from your hair and face. Wash your hands thoroughly with soap after using the restroom, and as often as possible after clearing soiled dishes or handling money.

Check your total appearance in the mirror before you start work. Ask yourself, "If I owned a restaurant myself, would I give myself a job?"

■■■ YOUR ROLE IN THE RESTAURANT ORGANIZATION

The employees in a restaurant are organized into a chain-of-command or organizational structure. Employees are assigned activities in such a way that no work is duplicated or omitted. Their united activities are necessary to reach the goals of the establishment. The goals of a restaurant organization are to satisfy the customers and make a profit.

A server's job is to assist the management in reaching the goals by cooperating and working with the organization—giving good service, being efficient, avoiding waste, attending to safety and sanitation, and following the rules and regulations set up by management. Employees are expected to perform their jobs and help support coworkers in a team approach. This bonding of efforts will give the guests the best service. Remember, no one will have a job if the restaurant does not achieve its goals.

Knowing how you fit into the organization helps you have the proper attitude toward your job. The owner or owners are at the top of the orga-

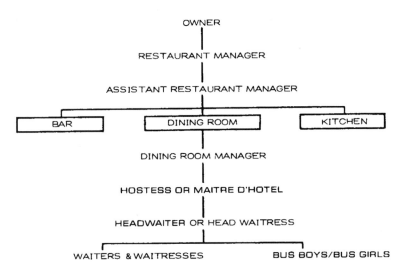

Figure 1-2   The relationship of the personnel in a traditional dining room is shown in this organizational chart.

nizational structure. The manager and assistant manager usually have authority over the bar, dining room, and kitchen. In the dining room, the hostess and maître d'hôtel may report to a dining room manager, and the head waitress and headwaiter may report to the hostess or maître d'hôtel. Waiters and waitresses usually report to their immediate supervisor, who may be a head waitress or headwaiter. Busboys and busgirls assist the servers. In small restaurants, several of these positions may be assumed by the same person. For instance, your immediate supervisor may be a maître d'hôtel or hostess who also assumes the head server's job. Figure 1–2 shows a traditional organizational structure in a restaurant.

To avoid causing problems within the organization, follow the organizational structure. When you have questions or problems concerning the rules, regulations, or policies, talk to your immediate supervisor. Your supervisor has more experience and is in a position to solve certain problems.

■■■■ TEAMWORK WITH COWORKERS AND SUPERVISORS

Teamwork means cooperating and working together with coworkers and the supervisor of the dining room to serve the public. A serving team is like a football team working toward a common goal. Whether the goal is a touchdown or a satisfied customer, the principles are the same.

Arrive at work with a positive attitude. Leave your personal problems at home and do not discuss them with coworkers or guests. Be cheerful and happy in your work; this attitude spreads to other workers and to the guests. Remember, guests come to the restaurant to relax and enjoy a special occasion in pleasant surroundings. If you have problems on the job, work them out or discuss them with your supervisor instead of with coworkers. Work can be pleasant or unpleasant depending on your attitude toward it.

Avoid raising your voice to any coworker or the chef when problems arise. Instead, try to handle the situation calmly. Some managers will train you in other jobs (chef, busperson, host) or allow you to experience other positions to build empathy with coworkers. Remember, you are a professional and a representative of the restaurant, and you should handle problems with coworkers in a professional manner.

Give coworkers assistance when they need help and you are not busy. For example, help them carry trays of food when they are serving an especially large party. If a guest in a coworker's station asks you for service, either cheerfully render the service or inform the guest's server. As a member of the team, coworkers should return the favor when you are busy.

Refrain from chatting or gossiping with coworkers in the dining room. Your responsibility lies with your guests when you are on duty. If you have spare time, use it productively to check your station, polish glasses, fill condiment container, and replenish the sidestand.

If you are ill, notify your supervisor as soon as possible. Absenteeism without proper notification may mean that a coworker must assume double duty if a replacement is unobtainable.

If even one member of your restaurant's team falls short of his or her duties, it creates a ripple effect. It puts pressure on everyone. The outcome affects the entire operation.

▮▮▮▮ CURRENT ISSUES REGARDING RESTAURANT EMPLOYMENT

Current issues in restaurant employment include cultural diversity, harassment, violence, safety, and sanitation. Some of these issues are covered more thoroughly in other chapters, but deserve mention here.

ACCEPTING THE CULTURAL DIVERSITY OF ALL PEOPLE

The law states that every server, regardless of race, religion, or nationality, deserves to work in a safe and pleasant environment. Intolerance for coworker's differences will undermine the team effort necessary to serve the public well. Likewise, every guest should have equal treatment. Guests will have different tastes and these differences deserve to be respected. The server's conduct must be tolerant and respectful. Noncompliance could be cause for dismissal from your job because no restaurant wants to be labeled as racist or sexist and risk a lawsuit.

PREVENTING HARASSMENT ON THE JOB

Employees all have the legal right to a work environment free of verbal or physical harassment based on race, color, creed, religion, national origin, sex, sexual orientation, disability, age, marital status, status with regard to public assistance, veteran status, or any belief or attribute unrelated to job performance. One form of harassment, sexual harassment, is defined as unwelcome sexual advances, requests for sexual favors, and other verbal or physical conduct of a sexual nature. Sexual harassment creates stress, cuts productivity, and violates employee rights.

If you are harassed on the job follow these guidelines:

1. Explain to the person doing the harassing that it is objectionable to you and that you would like it stopped.

2. If it does not stop, report the offender to your immediate supervisor, or to his or her supervisor if he or she is the offender. Some restaurants have a telephone hot line for this purpose.

3. If using the internal complaint procedure does not correct the problem, file a formal complaint with your state department that deals with human rights or the Equal Employment Opportunities Commission.

The management of most restaurants have a zero-tolerance policy that states they will not tolerate any acts of harassment, intimidation, or threats among their employees. If reported, most offenders will be investigated discreetly and fairly. Management should take appropriate action whether it be against innocent injury or criminal intent to harm.

KEEPING VIOLENCE AND DRUGS OUT OF THE WORKPLACE

Everyone shares the responsibility for maintaining a safe work environment. When someone is acting strange, management should be advised. Unreported situations can have potentially violent consequences.

A potentially violent individual is usually someone who is depressed, a loner who intimidates those around him or her, or is lacking self-worth. It can often be a person who is a constant complainer or has a history of violence. Violence in the workplace may be a direct result of problems in the home. Studies of violence in the workplace indicate that drug or alcohol abuse is often a causing factor in the majority of violent incidents.

It is important to be drug-free as an employee. It is against the law to use illegal drugs. In addition, an employee using illegal drugs is involved in accidents on the job four times more often, needs sick leave twice as often, and is late for work three times more often than other employees. The server's conduct also detracts from his or her overall productivity and team goals.

SAFETY AND PREVENTING ACCIDENTS

Employees and management should work together to maintain a safe and secure restaurant environment. Servers should be alert to any hazards they encounter. Most accidents can be avoided if the problem is noticed and solved in time; for instance, immediate attention to remedy unsafe work routines, blocked exits, chipped or broken serviceware, and grease and food spills will prevent accidents involving these situations (see Chapter 6, Safety, Sanitation, and Emergency Procedures).

TAKING SANITATION SERIOUSLY

The serving team has almost as much contact with foods served to guests as the kitchen staff. It is of the utmost importance that servers adhere to strict sanitation guidelines when handling food or risk spreading diseases that could be distressing or life-threatening to guests. This includes washing hands and handling serviceware properly. Servers must be very conscientious in this regard. Sanitation guidelines and proper food handling techniques will be covered in depth in a future chapter (see Chapter 6, Safety, Sanitation, and Emergency Procedures).

QUESTIONS

1. What advantages of a serving position can you list other that those that are mentioned in Chapter 1?
2. What qualifications for a serving position can you name other than those mentioned in Chapter 1?
3. List all the ways a server of your gender can improve appearance, personal hygiene, and grooming for your job.
4. Why should a waiter or waitress have a knowledge of the chain-of-command of employees in a restaurant?
5. What part does teamwork play in the operation of a restaurant?
6. Why is it important to accept the cultural diversity of all coworkers and guests?
7. How can sexual harassment be avoided?
8. What is one way that you can reduce the possibility of a violent situation in the workplace?

PROJECTS

1. Design a waiter or waitress self-evaluation sheet as if you were the restaurant manager. List both personality and appearance qualifications for a serving position down the left side of the paper, and think of other qualifications you can add to those listed in the chapter. At the top of the right hand side, list a rating scale of poor, fair, good, and excellent. Rate yourself by checking the appropriate column for each qualification. Set a goal to improve yourself in all areas not marked good or excellent.
2. Observe the waiters or waitresses in a restaurant of your choice and note whether the appearance of the servers is satisfactory or unsatisfactory.
3. Draw an organizational chart of a restaurant of your choice. Indicate who would be your immediate supervisor if you were a server there, and why.
4. Have a group discussion and decide the best course of action to handle the following situations:
   a. The chef has made a mistake on your order.
   b. You have come down with a bad cold the night before you have to go to work.
   c. You are an above-average server and feel the policy of sharing tips equally with fellow workers is unfair.
5. Have a group discussion about the best plan of action to take in handling the following situation: A new employee has just begun to work in the restaurant.

She is a from another country and speaks with an accent. She needs to be accepted into the team. What can you, as a peer server, do to help her overcome any anxiety she may have?

2

TYPES OF TABLE SERVICE AND SETTINGS

Several different types of service are used in restaurants. Most types of service originated in the private homes of European nobility and over the years have been modified for restaurant use. Today each type retains particular distinguishing features, although some restaurants have combined features of two or more serving styles to accommodate the menu, facilities, and image of the restaurant. The four traditional types of service discussed in this chapter are French, Russian, English, and American. Other popular types of service explained in this chapter are the banquet, family-style, buffet, salad bars, oyster bars, dessert tables, and smorgasbord.

In addition to the distinguishing features, serving responsibilities, and advantages and disadvantages of different types of service, the table setting or cover of each is described. A *cover* is the arrangement of china, silverware, napkin, and glassware at each place setting.

■ FRENCH SERVICE

French service is a formal type of service originated for European nobility and presently enjoyed by the few who can afford the time and expense of meals served in this manner.

Figure 2-1 In French service, food is cooked in front of the guests on a small spirit stove. Two servers work together to serve the meal.

In French service, the food is cooked or completed at a side table in front of the guests (Figure 2–1). The food is brought from the kitchen to the dining room on heavy silver platters and placed on a cart called a guéridon. A small spirit stove called a réchaud is used to keep the food warm. The food is completed by cooking, deboning, slicing, and garnishing as necessary and served to the guests on heated plates. Only those foods that can be cooked, assembled, or completed in a reasonably short time are prepared in front of the guests. Typical specialties that may be served in the French style are La Salade César (Caesar salad), Le Tournedos au Poivre (pepper steak), and Les Crêpes Suzettes (crêpes in orange sauce).

French service employs two servers working together to serve the meal and may include a captain to seat guests and a wine steward to serve wine. The principal server is the *chef de rang* (or experienced server) who seats the guests when a captain is not present, takes the order, serves the drinks, prepares some of the food with flourish at the guests' table, and presents the check for payment. The assistant is the *commis de rang*, who takes the order from the chef de rang to the kitchen, picks up the food and carries it to the dining room, serves the plates as dished up by the chef de rang, clears the dishes, and stands ready to assist whenever necessary. All food is served and cleared from the right of the guests except for butter, bread, and salad, which should be placed to the left side of the guests.

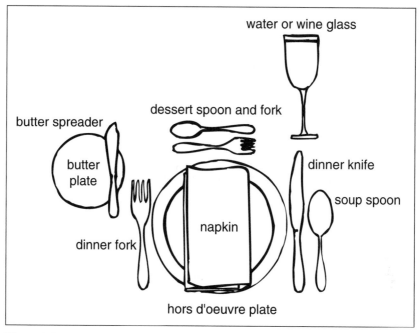

Figure 2-2 Serviceware in French service includes a butter plate, butter spreader, hors d'oeuvre plate, napkin, dinner fork, dinner knife, soup spoon, dessert fork and spoon, and water or wine glass.

Finger bowls—bowls of warm water with rose petals or lemon slices in them—are served with all finger foods (such as chicken and lobster) and at the end of the meal. The finger bowl is set on a doily on a small plate called an underliner and placed with a clean napkin in front of the guests.

Soiled dishes are cleared only when all guests have completed their meals.

FRENCH TABLE SETTING

The French cover includes an hors d'oeuvre plate (or show plate), napkin, dinner fork, dinner knife, soup spoon, butter plate, butter spreader, dessert fork and spoon, and water or wine glass. The French arrangement of serviceware is shown in Figure 2–2.

ADVANTAGES AND DISADVANTAGES OF FRENCH SERVICE

The advantages of French service are that guests receive a great deal of attention and the service is extremely elegant. The disadvantages are that fewer guests may be served, more space is necessary for service, many highly professional servers are required, and service is time-consuming.

■ RUSSIAN SERVICE

Russian service is similar to French service in many respects. It is very formal and elegant, and the guest is given considerable personal attention. It employs the use of heavy silver serviceware, and the table setting is identical to the French setup. The two major differences are that only one server is needed and that food is fully prepared and attractively arranged on silver platters in the kitchen.

To serve, the server places a heated plate before each guest from the right side, going around the table clockwise. Then the server brings the platters to the dining room from the kitchen and presents them to guests at the table.

Standing to the left of each guest and holding the platter of food in the left hand, the server shows each guest the food and then, using a large spoon and fork in the right hand, dishes up the desired portion on the guest's plate (Figure 2–3). The server continues serving counterclockwise around the table and then returns the unserved food to the kitchen. As in French service, finger bowls and napkins are served with the meal, and soiled dishes are cleared when all guests have completed the meal.

Figure 2-3   When serving food from a pan or platter, the server uses a serving spoon and fork in one hand to place food and juices on the guest's plate.

ADVANTAGES AND DISADVANTAGES
OF RUSSIAN SERVICE

The advantages of Russian service are that only one server is needed and service is as elegant as French service, yet faster and less expensive. No extra space is needed for special equipment, such as the guéridon.

The disadvantages of Russian service are the large investment in silver serviceware and the number of platters needed when every guest orders a different selection. For this reason Russian service is particularly useful at banquets where every guest receives the same food selection. Another disadvantage is that the last guest served at the table must be served from the less appetizing food remaining.

ENGLISH SERVICE

English service is used occasionally for a special dinner served in a private dining room of a restaurant, but it is more typical of a meal served by servants in a private home.

The food on platters and the heated plates are brought from the kitchen and placed before the host or hostess at the head of the table. The host or hostess, or one of the servers, carves the meat, if necessary, and dishes up the entrée and vegetable on individual plates. He or she hands the plates to the waiter standing to the left, who serves the guest of honor and all other guests. Dessert may also be served in this manner. All sauces and side dishes and, in some cases, the vegetables are on the table to be passed by the guests.

ADVANTAGES AND DISADVANTAGES
OF ENGLISH SERVICE

The advantage of English service is that it involves a great deal of showmanship for a special occasion. The disadvantages are that the host or hostess may be required to do a lot of the work by dishing up some of the food. With only one person serving the entrée, the service could be very time-consuming.

AMERICAN SERVICE

American service is less formal than French, Russian, or English service. It is the most prevalent style of service in restaurants in the United States.

In American service, food is dished up on plates in the kitchen. Except for the salad and the bread and butter, most of the food is placed on the entrée plate. Only one waiter or waitress serves the meal. Food is served from the left of the guest, beverages are served from the right, and soiled dishes are cleared from the right.

Figure 2-4   The initial American breakfast and lunch cover is set with a napkin, dinner fork, dinner knife, teaspoon, bread-and-butter plate, and water glass. An optional butter spreader may be placed on the bread and butter plate.

The American breakfast and lunch table setting differs from the American dinner setting. Breakfast and lunch are simple meals and require only a limited amount of serviceware. Dinner involves more courses and more serviceware.

American service can be simple and casual or complex and elegant. It can be used to serve the guest who wants a quick, filling meal at a casual restaurant with simple service. For instance, it can be used at a counter, diner, or family-style restaurant where casual tableware and placemats are the norm, and where self-serve bars such as salad bars are common. American service can also be used to serve the guest who intends to be entertained for the evening at a five-star establishment. It can be used to present food elegantly in distinguished gourmet restaurants with formal tablesettings and the use of complex serving skills and showmanship. The remainder of this manual explains American service in detail..

AMERICAN BREAKFAST AND LUNCH COVER

Serviceware for the American breakfast and lunch cover includes a dinner fork, dinner knife, teaspoon, napkin, bread-and-butter plate, butter spreader (optional), and water glass.

The breakfast and lunch cover is placed approximately one inch from the edge of the table. The napkin is in the center of the cover. To the left of the

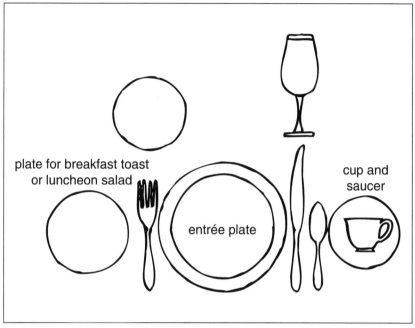

plate for breakfast toast
or luncheon salad

cup and
saucer

entrée plate

Figure 2-5   As food is served for the American breakfast or lunch, the dishes are placed in specific locations of the cover as diagrammed. The breakfast toast or luncheon salad is placed to the left of the fork, the entrée is centered, and the cup with saucer is placed to the right of the spoon.

napkin is the fork, and to the right of the napkin is the knife with the blade facing toward the napkin. The teaspoon is to the right of the knife. The water glass is placed above the tip of the knife. The bread-and-butter plate is placed above the tines of the fork. Traditionally, a small butter spreader was placed on the rim of the bread-and-butter plate, but today only a few restaurants use it. Figure 2–4 shows the initial American breakfast and lunch cover.

When coffee is served, the cup and saucer are placed to the right of the teaspoon. Breakfast toast or a luncheon salad is placed to the left of the fork. The entrée plate is placed directly in the center of the cover after the guest has removed the napkin. Side dishes and accompaniments are placed in a convenient location on the table when served. Figure 2–5 shows the place setting including the dishes served during the meal.

AMERICAN DINNER COVER

Serviceware for the American dinner cover includes two dinner forks, dinner knife, butter spreader, two teaspoons, service plate (optional), napkin, bread-and-butter plate, and water glass.

The dinner cover is placed approximately one inch from the edge of the table. The napkin is placed on a service plate or by itself in the center of the cover. The two dinner forks are to the left of the napkin. The dinner knife is to the immediate right of the napkin and then, in order, are the butter

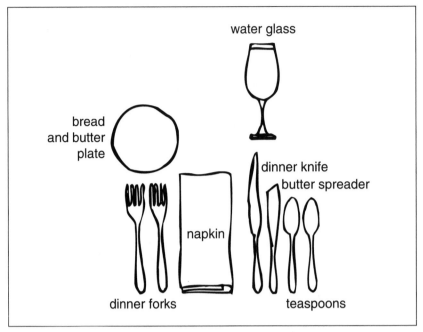

Figure 2-6 The initial American dinner cover includes a napkin, two dinner forks, dinner knife, butter spreader, two teaspoons, bread-and-butter plate, and water glass. An alternative cover is to have the butter spreader on the bread-and-butter plate.

spreader and two teaspoons. The blades of the knives face the napkin. The water glass is placed directly above the bread-and-butter spreader. The bread-and-butter plate is centered above the forks. An alternative American cover is to have the butter spreader placed on the bread and butter plate. The initial American dinner cover is shown in Figure 2–6.

When soup or an appetizer is ordered, it is placed on an underliner and served in the center of the cover. The salad is placed to the left of the forks, and coffee, when served, is placed to the right of the spoon. The entrée is placed in the center of the cover. Special-purpose silverware, such as the soup spoon with soup, is brought in as needed. Rolls, accompaniments, and side dishes are placed in convenient locations on the table. Diagrammed in Figure 2–7 is the place setting with the dishes served during the course of the meal.

■■■■ BANQUET SERVICE

Banquet service is serving a meal to a group of people who are celebrating, gathering for a special occasion, or honoring special guests. The menu, number of guests, and time of service is predetermined, and the banquet is well organized in advance (Figure 2–8).

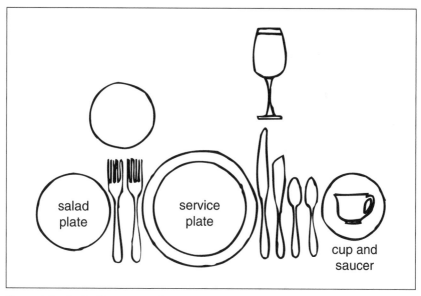

Figure 2-7   As the dinner is served using the American dinner cover, the salad is placed to the left of the forks, the entrée is centered, and the cup with saucer is placed to the right of the spoons.

Figure 2-8   A banquet setup features a head table for officials, speakers, and honored guests. The head table may be raised and centered to distinguish it from the other tables.

The waiter or waitress generally sets the tables with American settings modified according to the particular menu. For example, soup spoons or steak knives may be part of the initial cover if soup or steak is to be served. Occasionally French, Russian, or buffet service is used at the banquet, and the table is set accordingly.

If a cold course is planned, such as tomato juice, shrimp cocktail, or a salad, it is placed on the table just before the guests are seated. Also at this time, ice water is poured, butter pats are placed on the bread-and-butter plates, and baskets of hot rolls are arranged on the tables.

The food is put on plates in the kitchen and served to the guests in the usual American serving style (see Chapter 5, Serving the Meal) or served in French, Russian, or buffet style as predetermined. The head table is served first, then the rest of the tables. Water and coffee are refilled periodically.

If the guests will remain seated for entertainment or a speaker after dinner be sure the tables are cleared and tidy at the completion of the meal. Since the banquet is prepaid in advance, the server does not need to present a check or collect payment. The tip is often included in the contract made by the catering manager and the client arranging the banquet.

ADVANTAGES AND DISADVANTAGES OF BANQUET SERVICE

The advantages of the banquet service are that the menu and serving time are predetermined, which makes service a simple routine accomplished by fewer servers than with other types of serving. A disadvantage of banquet service is that guests receive very little personal attention. They are usually seated in close quarters, making proper service difficult.

◼ FAMILY-STYLE SERVICE

Family-style service is an informal modification of American service. All necessary preparation, such as cooking foods and slicing meats, is done in the kitchen. The food is then placed in large bowls and on platters and is properly garnished. The waiter or waitress serves the bowls and platters by placing them in the center of the table. The food is passed around the table by the guests, who help themselves to the portions desired.

The amount of service required of the waiter or waitress is minimized because the server simply sets the food on the table, pours the beverages, brings the appropriate condiments, and clears away the soiled dishes. Initial platters and bowls contain only enough servings for the number of guests in the party. If the family-style service has an all-you-can-eat feature, waiters and waitresses must refill serving containers when requested. Usually the American cover or a modification is used. Serving utensils are brought with the platters and bowls of food.

Figure 2-9 In the buffet service, the guests either help themselves from an attractive arrangement of food or are served by chefs standing behind the buffet table. A chef is usually responsible for carving meats.

ADVANTAGES AND DISADVANTAGES OF FAMILY-STYLE SERVICE

This simplified manner of service is advantageous to new servers who have not learned the proper details of serving. It is fast because the guests actually serve themselves; a waiter or waitress can serve more people than when a more formal type of service is used.

The disadvantages are that customers receive less personal attention and must serve themselves from a food platter that becomes less attractive as other guests serve themselves.

■ BUFFETS

With buffet service, guests select their meal from an attractive arrangement of food on long serving tables. The guests either help themselves or are served by chefs standing behind the buffet tables. Usually the service combines both types—the guests select relishes, salads, and vegetables themselves, and the meat is carved and served to the guests by chefs (Figure 2–9). Silverware and napkins may be conveniently located on the buffet table for the guests to pick up with their meal, or a complete cover (usually American) including rolls, butter, and condiments may be preset at the dining tables.

The job of the waiter or waitress varies, depending on the design of the buffet. The servers may serve only beverages and dessert, or they may serve several courses, such as the appetizer and soup, at the guest's tables. Remove soiled tableware and notify guests that they are to use clean plates each time they return to the buffet to maintain the sanitary condition of the buffet foods.

ADVANTAGES AND DISADVANTAGES OF BUFFET SERVICE

One advantage to buffet service is that food can be displayed in a very attractive manner. However, this can quickly become a disadvantage if care is not taken to keep the food selections fresh and complete. Another advantage is that servers can attend to many guests at one time, but guests receive less personal attention than in table service.

◼◼◼ SALAD BARS, OYSTER BARS, AND DESSERT TABLES

In other variations of buffets, only the salad, seafood appetizer, or dessert is served buffet style—the remainder of the meal is served in the usual manner.

SALAD BARS

A salad bar is a self-service concept in which each customer is given the opportunity to prepare his or her own salad from an attractive array of fresh vegetables and fruits that have been cleaned and sliced or quartered. Bowls and salad plates are available at one end of the salad bar. Guests prepare their own tossed green salads and help themselves to a variety of prepared salad accompaniments, such as salad dressings, crackers, and bread sticks.

More elaborate salad bars offer soups, pasta salads, cold cut vegetables, fruits, hard-boiled eggs, grated cheese, and crouton and seed toppings. And even more elaborate salad bars may include dishes such as pickled herring, sardines, thinly sliced ham, and tuna salad.

A clear, protective panel, called a *sneeze guard* or *food guard*, is mounted above the salad bar. Guests must also take a clean plate or bowl for each return trip. The sneeze guard and clean plate for refills ensure that salads are protected from contamination.

The duties of the waiter or waitress are first to take the guest's meal and wine order and then to inform them when and how to begin the salad bar. Remind guests they must use a clean plate each time they go to the salad bar for refills. Servers also assist the kitchen staff in the upkeep of the salad selections by informing them when food at the salad bar needs replenishing. Servers should remove soiled salad dishes from tables as they accumulate and keep beverages fresh during this course.

Figure 2-10   An oyster bar has seafood appetizers displayed attractively on a buffet table.

OYSTER BARS

An oyster bar is a buffet featuring oysters on the half shell and various seafood and mustard sauces that complement the oysters. Sometimes boiled shrimp and other appetizer seafoods extend the selection. The chef may want to display these foods in a nautical setting of shells, ice chips, nets, and diving relics to add to their appeal (Figure 2–10). An oyster bar is pictured in Figure 2–10.

DESSERT TABLES

A tantalizing display of tortes, pies, cakes, cream puffs, éclairs, fresh fruits, and soft cheeses displayed in buffet fashion constitutes a dessert table (Figure 2–11). Dessert plates and forks are at hand at the dessert table. Usually desserts are precut into portions, and guests help themselves.

Well-displayed desserts can also be brought to the guest's table on a tray or on a dessert cart with wheels. Servers bring the cart or tray at the end of the meal and can easily sell and serve portions from the selection at hand.

ADVANTAGES AND DISADVANTAGES OF SALAD BAR, OYSTER BAR, AND DESSERT TABLE SERVICES

As with conventional buffet service, the food at the salad and oyster bars and dessert table can be arranged very attractively. Less work is involved for the server because the customers take care of getting their own soup, salad, bread, appetizer, or dessert. The server has more time to serve many cus-

Figure 2-11   Dessert carts and tables feature a wide choice of tortes, pies, cakes, custards, and other sweets.

tomers, which increases opportunities for extra tips.

The disadvantage of salad or oyster bars or dessert tables is that, like the buffet, they must be replenished constantly to look attractive; otherwise, complaints may result. Also, the timing of the meal can be upset; the server must be able to coordinate the self-service of the customer at the salad or oyster bar with the rest of the meal.

Dessert carts or trays, unlike self-serve bars and tables, require more time on the part of the server. The waiter or waitress must push or carry them to the table, sell, and serve the desserts.

SMORGASBORDS

A smorgasbord is a buffet featuring a large selection of food with many Scandinavian selections, such as cheese and herring. In many places it is a set-price, self-service buffet of any kind of food. Usually guests may come back to the smorgasbord table and refill their plates as often as they desire. The basic discussion of buffets also applies to smorgasbords.

 QUESTIONS

1. Define *cover* and *underliner.*
2. Why do very few restaurants use French service?
3. How are French service and Russian service alike? How do they differ?
4. When is English service used today?
5. Why is American service used in most restaurants today?
6. Why is American service sometimes called "plate service?"
7. How is the banquet setup prior to the seating of guests?
8. What is the distinguishing feature of family-style service?
9. How are buffets, salad bars, oyster bars, dessert tables, and smorgasbords similar? How do they differ from one another?
10. From your experience, give examples of how two types of service are used together.

 PROJECTS

1. Make a chart for the nine types of service discussed in this chapter. List the types of service down the left margin. Across the top of the chart, label the vertical columns with the following headings: Distinguishing Features, Server's Responsibilities, Advantages, Disadvantages. Complete the chart by using information from this chapter.
2. Using proper serviceware, set up the American breakfast and lunch cover and the American dinner cover. In a training session, point out similarities and differences between the settings. Identify the purpose of each serviceware piece, and show the placement of various foods as they are served.
3. Observe different types of service in various restaurants, and discuss with other trainees what you have learned.

3

BEFORE THE GUESTS ARRIVE

Waiters and waitresses have many responsibilities to attend to prior to serving any guests in a restaurant. They are first assigned the tables at which their guests will eat. They must then attend to sidework. *Sidework* is a term designating all the duties the waiter or waitress performs other than those directly related to serving the guests. Sidework includes the opening duties, such as preparing the dining room and studying the menu, as well as leaving the work area in proper order upon completion of the shift.

▌ STATION ASSIGNMENTS

A *station* is a section of the dining room assigned as a work area to a waiter or waitress. Each station has seating for about a dozen or more guests at tables, booths, or counters. Ideally, a dining room should be divided into stations that are equal to one another in the number of people they seat, in the distance from sidestands and kitchen, and in desirability of seats to the guests. Of course, this balance is impossible in most dining rooms because there will always be less desirable seats near kitchen and washroom entrances and away from scenic views.

Because stations are not equally desirable from a seating and serving standpoint, dining room managers often assign stations to waiters and waitresses on a rotational basis—servers take turns from day to day serving in the best stations.

In some restaurants, servers with seniority have permanent stations that are larger or more desirable than others. This assignment is made because these servers are experienced and can handle more guests and because certain customers request a particular server and seat. The new waiter or waitress may be assigned a less desirable station, which provides an opportunity to gain experience with a smaller number of guests.

For convenience, tables are often numbered and stations are assigned by giving the numbers of the tables to a waiter or waitress. The server then uses these numbers on orders and guest checks to identify the party of guests being served.

◼ DINING ROOM PREPARATION

PREPARING THE TABLES

The first opening duty is to check your station to see that the general area is presentable and ready to setup for service. Setup enough tables to accommodate the reservations and the average number of persons without reservations who are expected.

Using a clean cloth or sponge rinsed in sanitizing solution, thoroughly wash the tables before you set them. Check the seats, dusting off crumbs and cleaning sticky areas. If tablecloths are used, select the appropriate size and spread the cloth on the table so that all four corners hang evenly and the edges of the tablecloth are just touching the seats of the chairs (Figure 3–1). Often a pad or second tablecloth called a *silencer* is placed beneath the top cloth. The silencer gives the table a better appearance and softens the clanking noise of the serviceware.

A professional way of placing the cloth on the table is to place a centerfold on the center of the table and to open the cloth to cover the table top. This method assures a quick, well-centered placement of the cloth. It may be used to replace soiled cloths while guests are present.

When condiments, candles, and flowers are on the table and the soiled cloth must be changed, move the items to one half of the tablecloth. Gather up the soiled cloth, exposing one half of the table or silencer, and then place the center items on the table or silencer. Enclosing the crumbs so they do not fall on the seats and floor, remove the rest of the soiled cloth completely.

Replacing the cloth is the reverse operation. With center items remaining at the edge of the table, place the centerfold of the tablecloth at the center of the table. Fold up the top half so the center items may be placed on the surface of the cloth. Then open the cloth completely and arrange the condiments, centerpieces, and other items (Figure 3–2). If placemats are used, arrange them neatly on the clean tables.

After the tablecloths or placemats are arranged properly, set up the covers. A cover consists of china, silverware, napkins, and glassware at each

Figure 3-1   The proper way of arranging the tablecloth is so that the edges of the cloth just touch the chairs. Guests approaching the table get a favorable impression of the meal to come as they observe the even arrangement of the cloth, napkins, and place settings.

place setting. The amount of serviceware and the arrangement depend on the type of service and the meal to be served (see Chapter 2, Types of Table Service and Settings).

Carry supplies of chinaware, glassware, silverware, and napkins to the table on clean trays. Handle china by the edges, glassware by the bases or stems, and silverware by the handles as you set up covers. Set aside any serviceware that is damaged or soiled, and return it to the kitchen. Glasses and cups should be inverted until the time of service, but be sure the glasses are inverted on only clean tablecloths and placemats so the rims remain sanitary. Discard any chipped or cracked glassware or china immediately.

After the covers have been set, check to see that all centerpieces are fresh and clean, that candles are replaced, or that lights are in working order. When table tent menus—small menus designed to stand vertically—are used, place them uniformly on all tables.

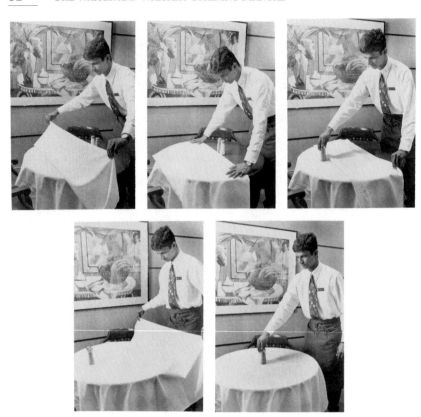

Figure 3-2   Placing the cloth on the table is illustrated: 1. with salt, pepper, or vase moved to the edge, place the center fold of the cloth on the table; 2. position the cloth so it drapes evenly; 3. open the cloth and gently gather or fold it up at the center of the table, and transfer the salt, pepper, or vase to the half already spread; 4. spread the cloth over the remainder of the table; 5. center the condiments or vase.

PREPARING THE SIDESTAND

A *sidestand* is a storage and service unit located close to serving areas (Figure 3–3). It eliminates the need for waiters and waitresses to make frequent trips to the kitchen for supplies. One of the main opening duties is to stock the sidestand nearest your station with serviceware, garnishes, beverages, and supplies. The items kept in stock at the sidestand vary among restaurants. Typical sidestand supplies include:

- Coffee warmers with fresh coffee
- Ice tongs
- Clean ashtrays and matches

Figure 3-3 A sidestand like this placed close to serving areas puts items needed in easy distance of the guests and reduces the number of trips that must be made to the kitchen.

- Clean, folded napkins
- Sponges and towels
- Order pads, guest checks, and extra pencils
- Condiments such as salt, pepper, steak sauce, catsup, mustard, and seasoning salt in clean, filled containers
- Meal accompaniments, such as lemon wedges, coffee cream, horseradish, and jelly or preserves according to the menu of the day (see the section on Meal Accompaniments later in this chapter)
- Clean placemats
- Children's placemats, menus, bibs, and favors
- Silver and supplies for special food items, such as lemon squeezers, straws, iced tea spoons, and seafood forks
- Clean menus
- Drink coasters or napkins
- Tip trays or tip wallets
- China, silver, and glasses to set up covers

Because the sidestand is in plain view of the guests, it must be clean, neat, and presentable at all times. During the course of service, busboys or busgirls should be notified to replace low inventories of supplies if you are too busy to replace them on your return trips from the kitchen.

▮ STUDYING THE MENU

WHY STUDY THE MENU?

Familiarizing yourself with the menu should be one of your daily responsibilities. Study the menu so that you are aware of any changes in food choices and prices from day to day. Study the menu to learn all the menu items offered so you can sell foods that will be appealing to the customer and suggest side dishes. And know the menu so that you can answer the guest's questions. Following are reasons why you should study the menu:

1. Study the menu frequently because it may change occasionally or even daily. Check with the chef if you see any new specials or menu items. Selections may change to give variety to the menu, and prices may change according to ingredient cost or seasonal availability of food items.

2. Know about the food on the menu so you can sell it to the guests. Consider yourself a salesperson and the menu items your product. Know the menu so you can describe the foods accurately and help guests make satisfying choices. Knowing the menu helps you suggest side orders and build the check. For instance, suggest a la carte items that complement the entrées chosen or additional foods that round out the meal or add to the festivity of the occasion, such as appetizers, champagne, or dessert.

3. Be knowledgeable about food items so you can help those customers who request information that may not be on the menu. For instance, you many have to answer questions about vegetarian selections, budget-wise choices, kosher foods, food ingredients that may cause allergies, healthy choices, or foods for finicky eaters. With a knowledge of food ingredients and prices you can help guests who have questions about the following:

   - *Vegetarian foods*   Know whether foods contain white meats or are without meat altogether.

   - *Budget-wise selections*   Know which items give you the best value for your money.

   - *Kosher food*   Know if any of the menu items are prepared under strict kosher rules and with kosher ingredients (see the section on Content of the Menu later in this chapter).

   - *Ingredients that may cause allergic reactions*   There are guests who are allergic to shrimp, dairy products, or eggs. A gluten-restricted diet may prevent some guests from eating foods with wheat, rye, barley, or oat derivatives. Monosodium glutamate and some forms of hydrolyzed vegetable protein can be a problem for a few of your guests. Know the exact ingredients in menu foods and how they are prepared.

- *Healthy choices* A guest may be diabetic and must know the sugar content in prepared foods. Some people may be on low-calorie or low-fat diets and want to know how foods are cooked or want to know if they can get sauces "on the side" so they may add them sparingly.

- *Foods they may dislike* For example, small children may not like foods such as onions or nuts.

Knowing the menu items in great detail will help you make suggestions and answer questions. If you do not know ingredients in foods, do not guess. Ask the chef for the exact ingredients so that your guests can make informed choices.

TYPES OF MENUS

The most common menus are those for breakfast, lunch, and dinner. Usually each meal has a separate menu, but occasionally a single menu contains selections for all three meals. The menu that is exclusively for luncheons contains sandwiches and light entrées. The dinner menu (Figure 3–4) contains entrées of larger portions, "heavier" foods like steaks and chops, and additional accompaniments such as vegetables. More food naturally causes the prices on dinner menus to be higher.

In addition to regular menus there are menus for wines called wine lists (see Chapter 8, Wine and Bar Service) and table tent menus that note particular items like specials, unusual drinks, or a dessert of the day. Blackboard menus, menus written on a blackboard at the entrance to some restaurants, are also in use. Servers in these restaurants memorize the menu and repeat it to guests from memory instead of issuing paper menus.

There are children's menus with children's favorite foods, speedy service, child-size portions, and lower prices. These menus are very important for parents wishing to dine out with their children.

When food on a menu is a la carte, it is listed as a single item and priced separately from other foods. A sandwich listing is characteristic of this type of menu selection. When food on a menu is table d'hôte, it is listed as a full-course meal and is priced as a unit that may include soup, rolls, salad, entrée, potato, and vegetable. Most menus contain an assortment of foods in both a la carte and table d'hôte listings.

CONTENT OF THE MENU

The content of the menu is organized into categories, or food groups, and also features specials. The categories, specials, and trends in foods presented are discussed below.

Categories. The foods on menus are grouped into categories according to the customs and preferences of management. Some of the more popular categories are:

Welcome to Historic Madison and the Key West Shrimp House

You have shown distinguished good taste in selecting Madison's finest restaurant. Now sit back and relax. You are in for a real treat.

The Captain's Table

The number one choice of the house, served in five courses, A Key West Shrimp House exclusive.

1. Anchors Aweigh A crispy chilled shrimp cocktail with a tangy, tasty sauce.

2. Underway A cup of the famous Key West chowder and salad bar.

3. Half-Speed A steaming portion of crab legs and ocean-fresh shrimp, and scallops.

4. Full Speed Ahead Another steaming platter, but this time comprised of French fried shrimp, frog leg, and ocean-fresh fish.

5. Port Of Call Slow down, now, and enjoy your culinary cruise with some whiskey pudding with our special sauce or Key Lime pie.

24.95

Your choice of a 1/2 Carafe of Rose, Chablis or Burgunday wine.

With Your Dinner

SELECT ONE OF THE FOLLOWING

Individual serving of assorted vegetables, steamed in butter, lemon and cheese.

Chef's bean casserole, A mixture of butter, kidney and great northern beans. Properly prepared and seasoned to please all bean lovers.

Potatoes/french fried, twice baked or rice.

Most dinners except Lite Appetite served with onion boullion and Salad Bar.
All dishes are prepared WHEN ORDER IS RECEIVED IN OUR KITCHENS.

Appetizers

Shrimp Cocktail	6.50
Seafood Chowder	Cup 2.50 Bowl 3.95
Fried Onion Thins	3.00
Stuffed Jalapeno Peppers	3.25
Mozzarella Sticks	3.25
Peel & Eat Shrimp - served cold or hot	7.95

Combinations

Steak & Lobster	(Market)	Steak & Shrimp ... 17.95
Steak & Crab	(Market)	Steak & Halibut ... 17.95
Lobster & Shrimp	(Market)	Steak & Broiled Chicken Breast .. 15.95

Special combinations available upon request.

Figure 3-4 A typical dinner menu contains many categories of related a la carte (individually priced) or table d'hôte (complete dinner) selections.

Chicken

Stir Fried Chicken

Gently stir fried with onions, green pepper, mushrooms and original Key West sauce. Served on a
bed of rice. Guaranteed to satisfy any appetite.   12.95

Broiled Chicken Breast

Seasoned in special sauce, then placed under the broiler.   12.95

Chicken Alfredo

Broiled chicken breast served over a bed of fettuccini, topped with white creamy alfredo sauce.

13.95

Steak

Steaks Aristocratique ....

The quality of our steaks is top choice, broiled to your specifications.

We cannot be responsible for well done steaks.

5 oz. Steak - 12.95   8 oz. Filet - 16.95   10 oz. Rib Eye - 13.95

Lite Appetite

THE DINNERS LISTED HERE Include Salad with your choice of dressing and a choice of
French Fried Potatoes or Rice.

French Fried Shrimp (4) 9.95	Panama (5) 9.95
Steamed-In—A-Net 9.95	French Fried Fish 9.45
Crab Legs .... (Market Price)	Scallops, French Fried........... 9.95
Same triple A quality served on our regular dinners.	We use the bay scallop for flavor and tenderness.
Small Steak..................... 10.95	Baked Fish, In Casserole 9.45
U.S. Choice quality.	Fish will be served in individual casserole, baked in butter and lemon, or if you prefer - lightly covered with Panama sauce.
Seafood Norfolk................. 10.95	
This favorite is fully described in the first section.	

Desserts

We serve all homemade desserts. The
desserts available change daily. Please
ask your server to see our selection of
homemade desserts.

Closed Monday

Tuesday - Friday	Saturday	Sunday
Lunch 11-2	11-2	Noon-8
Evening 5-9	Evening 5-10	

Figure 3-4 (con't)

Shrimp

Coconut Shrimp

Definitely one of the House specialties. Our large Shell Pink Shrimp is freshly prepared for each order. After dipping in a light liquid, the shrimp is rolled in chopped coconut, then carefully french fried to protect the flavor.   14.95

Shrimp, French Fried

This is the dish that made the Key West Shrimp House famous. Back in 1950 when the old original Key West Shrimp House first opened, this was the only item on the menu...and it is still one of the most popular.

These beautiful Shrimp are peeled, hand breaded, flavored with spices and herbs, then French-fried to a golden, crispy brown. At first taste you will know why they made us famous.   14.95

Shrimp Panama

From the interior of the historic Republic of Panama came this recipe. The Shrimp are peeled, pre-boiled, rolled in bacon, and then simmered in a secret sauce that givers them that special flavor. "Muy Delicioso."   13.95

Chef's Special

No doubt the favorite of all those who are regulars. Combination Shrimp Panama and French Fried Shrimp.   14.95

Shrimp Broiled

These large delicious shrimp are split, brushed with butter and other delicate seasonings, then placed under the broiler; fantastic.   14.95

Shrimp-In-A-Net

These delightful Shrimp are placed in a fish net and submerged for exactly four minutes in boiling and seasoned liquid. Served to you in the net, you peel them and dip them in the zesty Key West sauce for a dining delight.   13.95

Seafood Norfolk

A triple-feature favorite of Key West Shrimp House regulars for years. Scallops, shrimp, lobster meat, sea legs chopped to blend...simmered and served en casserole with pure creamery butter.
                    14.95

Alaskan King Crab Legs

Preparation makes the big difference with this dish and we have been doing it since the 1950's.
(Market Price)

Lobster

The market in lobster varies almost from day to day throughout the world. We select only the very best from whatever is available. But whatever the Key West Shrimp House serves will be delectable.
(Ask your waitress)

Seafood Platter

A combination of french fried shrimp, scallops, fish, frog leg, and clam strips.   14.95

Shrimp Scampi

Peeled, and split, brushed with lemon, butter and garlic, then placed under the broiler.   15.95

Figure 3-4 (con't)

Fish

Halibut Oscar, Baked

The Choice of Kings. A meaty white fish, smothered in hollandaise sauce and garnished with asparagus.   13.95

Halibut, Broiled

Broiled in butter with special seasonings.   12.95

Stuffed Sole Monteray

Sole stuffed with a tasty combination of Crab, Bay Shrimp and Monteray Cheese.   12.95

The Beachcomber

White Fish served over a seasoned bed of rice and vegetables, topped with butter and sliced almonds. Soup and Salad Bar.   11.95

Fish, Deep Fried

Before frying, preparation is the determining factor as to how the end product will turn out. Sprinkled with fresh lemon juice and lightly breaded in a tasty different mixture of seasonings.
                                                                                                                                 10.95

Fish, Baked

Fish will be served in individual casserole, baked in butter and lemon, or if you prefer - lightly covered with Panama Sauce.   10.95

Filet Catfish, Deep Fried

The tremendous and growing demand for this fresh-water delicacy has created an entirely new industry called "Catfish Farming." The fingerlings are raised in acre-size ponds and fed a balanced, controlled diet to assure their growth to plump goodness. Each medium size fish is rolled in a light breading mixture, blended with seasoning herbs and spices, then crisply deep-fried.   10.95

Scallops in Wine Sauce

This seafood delicacy is becoming more popular for its flavor and tenderness in a wide variety of dishes. Simmered in seasoned wine and butter sauce in a Casserole.   14.95

Scallops, Deep Fried

14.95

Deep Fried Frog Legs

Lightly spiced. The history relating to the popularity of Frog Legs dates back to the Roman Legions. It will always be a favorite for those who demand the finest.   13.95

Ocean Scramble - When In Season

A steaming portion of shrimp, slipper lobster, crab legs, and clams served to you in a net.   16.95

Figure 3-4 (con't)

- An appetizer category includes foods served as a first course to stimulate the appetite of the guests. In a traditional restaurant, appetizers include small portions of juices, fruits, pâtés, and seafood items. The appetizer category in less formal restaurants is often dominated by finger foods and foods of ethnic origin or influence, such as nachos and pizza, and meant to be shared by several guests at the table.

- Soups may be placed in a separate category, grouped with appetizers, or included with table d'hôte entrées. Soups may be clear, cream-based, or cold.

- Salads, lightly tossed fresh greens, are grouped with soups, by themselves in a category, or featured with the main part of the meal.

- Entrées, the main part of the meal, can vary extensively and can be grouped in any number of categories. Some of the more common categories are steaks, seafood, meats, poultry, sandwiches, salads, and specialties. Generally, a vegetable and some type of starch accompany the meat entrées, but sometimes the entrée is featured by itself.

- The dessert category usually includes pies, cakes, ice cream, sherbet, sundaes, and specialties of the area. The dessert usually brings the meal to completion.

- The category of beverages includes coffee, tea, milk, soft drinks, and other drinks. Cocktails and wines may also be listed on the food menu.

The types of foods and the number of selections in each category vary from one restaurant to another. Exclusive restaurants list gourmet-type foods and family restaurants list home-style foods. Restaurants may list calories of each item, feature kosher foods, or identify low-fat or low-salt for healthy selections. Some restaurants still feature a large number of selections and others have followed the current trend toward limiting choices to cut costs.

Specials.   A special of the day may be attached to the menu. A special is a leftover, a regional or seasonal dish, or a chef's specialty. Bratwurst in Wisconsin or gumbo in Louisiana are regional specials. Fresh strawberries or melon or some seafoods are seasonal specials. A seasonal special is attached to the menu when an abundant supply of a particular food is available at a low price. A chef's special is a dish that the chef prepares exceptionally well.

Usually the price of the special is low if it is a leftover or a seasonal item. You should not mention that the special is a leftover or made from leftovers, because customers will feel the food selection is inferior. Instead, strive to describe specials in an appetizing way to increase sales. Remember, the product may taste as good or better than when it was first prepared if it is properly handled by the chef.

Trends.   Current trends affect the content of the menu. Specialty coffees like espresso-based lattes, cappuccinos, mochas, and Americanos have been growing in popularity. Also popular are bagels, chicken sandwiches, extra-large beverages, spicy foods, and meatless dishes.

Some restaurants may be setup to serve kosher foods and will indicate they are a kosher restaurant on the menu. Kosher foods are foods that are permitted to be eaten by people of the Jewish faith who observe kosher dietary laws. Kosher is a set of rules regarding preparation of foods with kosher ingredients in a kosher facility (or kitchen). Food that is kosher must be supervised during preparation and made with ingredients that are approved by certifying supervisors. The kosher consumer extends beyond the Jewish community to include Seventh Day Adventist, Moslems, vegetarians, and many health-conscious Americans. People with allergies to pork or shellfish will select kosher foods to avoid allergic reactions. People who are lactose intolerant can eat foods that are certified kosher and *parve*, which means without dairy products.

The increasing ethnic diversity of the United States will accelerate the trend toward more ethnic restaurants and ethnic dishes on the menus. Guests will enjoy unique menu choices such as Szechuan Chinese, Hunan Chinese, German, Greek, Japanese, Tex-Mex, Cajun-Creole, Mexican, Thai, Mandarin, and Italian.

METHODS OF FOOD PREPARATION

Because guests often ask how foods on the menu are prepared, you should know the more common preparation methods, as follows:

- *Baked*   Cooked by dry, continuous heat in an oven
- *Boiled*   Cooked in liquid at the boiling temperature of 212°F at sea level, so that bubbles rise to the surface and break
- *Braised*   Browned in a small amount of fat and then cooked slowly in a little liquid in a covered pan
- *Broiled*   Cooked by direct heat, either under the source of heat, as in a broiler, or over the source of heat, as on a grill
- *Fried*   Cooked in hot fat. Pan-fried and sautéed mean cooked in a small amount of fat. Deep-fried means cooked while immersed in a large amount of fat.
- *Grilled*   Cooked over direct heat, usually hot coals
- *Pan-broiled*   Cooked in a heavy frying pan over direct heat, using little or no fat
- *Poached*   Simmered in enough liquid to cover the food
- *Roasted*   Cooked uncovered without water added, usually in an oven
- *Sautéed*   Browned or cooked in a small amount of hot fat
- *Simmered*   Cooked gently in a liquid over low heat just below the boiling point
- *Steamed*   Cooked in steam with or without pressure
- *Stewed*   Simmered slowly in enough liquid to cover the food

PREPARATION TIME

Preparation time is the time required to cook and dish up a food item on the menu. It depends on the equipment in the kitchen, the efficiency of the chef, and the number of orders already placed by other waiters and waitresses. Preparation times can best be learned by experience. Once you know them, however, you will be able to time your orders competently.

Some of the more common food preparation times are as follows:

- *Eggs*   Ten minutes
- *Fish, fried or broiled*   10–15 minutes
- *Liver*   15 minutes
- *Chateaubriand*   30 minutes
- *Steak, one-inch thick*
  rare   Ten minutes
  medium   15 minutes
  well-done   20 minutes
- *Lamb chops*   20 minutes
- *Pork chops*   15–20 minutes
- *Game*   30–40 minutes
- *Fried chicken*   10–20 minutes
- *Soufflé*   35 minutes

New equipment and preparation methods have shortened preparation times considerably. Some foods are precooked in advance and heated to serving temperature when ordered. Other foods are prepared early in the day and kept at serving temperature constantly either on a steam table, if served hot, or in a refrigerator, if served cold. Equipment such as the microwave oven (Figure 3–5) shortens the preparation time of food items to minutes and seconds. For the customer's convenience during rush hours, know which items can be served to them immediately.

MEAL ACCOMPANIMENTS

Meal accompaniments are condiments, decorative garnishes, and foods that complement the entrée. Part of your responsibility may be bringing the condiments to the table to complete the order and adding the garnishes and complementary foods to an entrée prepared by the chef. Make sure the garnishes look attractive and that condiment containers are clean. Some accompaniments may be kept at the sidestand for convenience. Examples of meal accompaniments are as follows:

- Lemon wedge with fish
- Tartar sauce with fish

Figure 3-5   Food preparation of many items can be shortened considerably with the use of equipment like the microwave oven shown here.

- Catsup and pickles with hamburger
- Steak sauce with steak
- Mustard with hot dogs
- Applesauce with potato pancakes
- Syrup with pancakes
- Dressing with salads
- Butter with bread and rolls
- Crackers with soup
- Clarified butter with lobster
- Parsley to add color to an entrée
- Cream, sugar, and artificial sweetener with coffee
- Lemon, sugar, and artificial sweetener with tea

■ CLOSING THE DINING ROOM

Servers have closing duties to perform between luncheons and dinners and also at the end of the day. When closing after lunch, reset enough tables for the anticipated number of dinner guests.

At the end of the day, take the time to close the dining room properly. Leave your station, sidestand, and kitchen area in a clean, orderly condition, ready for business the next day. The following are some closing duties:

- To avoid a fire, collect all ashtrays from the tables and empty them into a fireproof container.

- Make sure the mouths of catsup bottles are wiped clean, and cruets are grease-free.

- Remove all salt, pepper, and sugar containers and place them on trays. Wipe the containers with a clean, damp cloth and refill them. Containers should be periodically emptied and washed.

- Take all condiments, such as catsup, mustard, and steak sauce, to the refrigerator.

- Cream and butter, if it has not been placed on individual bread-and-butter plates, should be emptied into large containers. The butter may be used in cooking.

- Strip the tables of their tablecloths. Tables should not be set up for the next day because settings gather dust. Instead, assemble all the service-ware on trays for use the next morning, and cover it with napkins.

- Empty all coffee containers and have coffee equipment cleaned.

- Return unused and voided numbered guest checks to the supervisor.

- Turn off all heating equipment, such as roll warmers and coffee-making equipment.

 QUESTIONS

1. Define *station, sidestand, silencer,* and *special.*
2. List several methods of assigning stations to servers and the reasons different methods of assignment are used.
3. Why do the amount and arrangement of serviceware in a cover vary?
4. Recommend a procedure for keeping the sidestand replenished on a routine basis.
5. Discuss the advantages and disadvantages of cabinet doors for concealing the shelves of sidestands.
6. Why is studying the menu necessary?
7. List several special problems people may have with certain foods on the menu.

8. List various ethnic menus or foods on a menu that are of ethnic origin.

9. Compare the job of a salesperson in a retail store with the job of a waiter or waitress. In what ways are their jobs alike? In what ways do they differ?

10. What are the main differences between the luncheon and the dinner menus?

11. Discuss several reasons why restaurants have specials on their menus. Why should servers suggest specials to their guests?

12. Why should a server be familiar with methods of food preparation and preparation times?

13. Why may preparation times vary from one restaurant to another?

 PROJECTS

1. List the opening duties for your restaurant or a local restaurant, and divide them among the servers who work the morning hours. You may want to rotate groups of duties so the waiters and waitresses can be responsible for a variety of jobs on different days.

2. Ask one trainee to demonstrate how to place a tablecloth on a table in a professional manner. Repeat this procedure with the center items on the table. Then have the trainee demonstrate how to remove the tablecloth with and without center items on the table. Have all trainees try this procedure.

3. Study several menus from local restaurants. Identify the following parts:

   a. Those items that are a la carte.

   b. Those items that are table d'hôte.

   c. The various groupings of foods and the number and kind of selections in each group.

   d. The special attachment or the place where a special may be attached.

4. Study a menu and consult with a chef in order to do the following:

   a. Identify the main ingredients of each food item.

   b. Describe the method of food preparation for each food item.

   c. Identify the preparation time necessary to cook or prepare each food item.

   d. Name the meal accompaniments that go with each food item.

5. Have a chef discuss how restaurant foods may be adapted to guest's special diet needs as they request.

6. List all the closing duties that you can think of or that must be done in your restaurant if you are already employed. Post these in the kitchen and make a regular habit of checking them off at the end of the day.

4

INITIATING THE SERVICE

Initiating the service means beginning the service. It includes greeting and seating the guests, taking the orders, timing the meal, and placing and picking up the orders in the kitchen. Appropriate conversation, answering questions, and making suggestions are also important parts of the initial service.

■ SEATING GUESTS

WHO SEATS GUESTS

Guests may be greeted and seated by the maître d'hôtel, hostess, headwaiter, or head waitress who keeps track of open tables, assigns waits, and seats people as their turn or reservation comes up. This process can make the guests feel immediately welcome and give them a good first impression of the restaurant. It also allows the maître d'hôtel or hostess to control the traffic flow of guests in the dining room by seating guests evenly among stations and staggering the seating. In some restaurants, however, guests are allowed to select their own table, booth, or counterspace.

WHERE TO SEAT GUESTS

Common sense dictates where parties of guests should be placed in the dining room. Utilize tables according to party size. For example, seat large families at large round tables and couples at smaller tables for two, called *deuces*.

Public health is protected by law. Clean indoor air statutes limit smoking to designated smoking areas of restaurants. These areas must be set aside from nonsmoking areas and posted for smoking. Seat smokers in smoking sections and nonsmokers away from them in nonsmoking sections.

Loud, noisy parties may be placed in private rooms or toward the back of the dining room so they do not disturb other guests. Elderly guests or guests with disabilities may wish to be near the entrance so they do not have far to walk. Young couples like quiet corners and good views. Of course, if guests request a specific location, try to accommodate them.

HOW TO SEAT GUESTS

Approach guests with words of greeting such as "Good evening." Guests will inform you when they have reservations. When they do not have reservations, ask them, "How many are in your party?" and "Would you like to be seated in a smoking or nonsmoking area?" When there appears to be one person, ask, "Table for one?" instead of "Are you alone?" If guests must wait for seating, take a name and tell them you will notify them when it becomes available. If there is dining seating available, take clean menus and lead the guests to the table.

When women are in the party, a maître d'hôtel or headwaiter seats one or more of them in the seats with the best view (Figure 4–1). Usually the men in the party assist in seating the other women present. A hostess or head waitress generally pulls out the women's chairs to indicate where they may be seated, but does not actually seat them. When patrons will be placed at wall tables with banquette seats on one side, the tables may be pulled away from the seats by the maître d'hôtel or hostess so guests may be seated easily. Open menus are presented to each guest, and friendly conversation is carried on throughout this initial service. At this time, remove table settings that will not be used, bring junior chairs or high chairs for children, and supply missing serviceware. Fill water glasses or have them filled by a busgirl or busboy.

CONTROLLING SEATING

To control the traffic flow in the restaurant, the greeter should avoid seating two groups of guests in the same station at the same time. Instead, seat parties in different stations so that a waiter or waitress is not overburdened with two new parties simultaneously and the guests receive better service. The greeter should also stagger the seating of large parties so that servers will have equal opportunities to serve large groups without having too many of these groups at one time.

On a busy day, many restaurants are so popular that guests have to wait for a table. The waiting areas can be mini-destination areas where guests

Figure 4–1   The maître d'hôtel or headwaiter seats the women in a party of guests although the men in the party may assist some of the women themselves.

enjoy first courses and beverages before moving into the dining room for the main course. Be sure guests are seated in order of their arrival and registration with you. Give preference to guests with reservations at their appointed times.

■ APPROACHING THE GUESTS

Approach the guests after they have had time to look at the menu. If they are seated by a maître d'hôtel or hostess, greet them with a friendly "Good evening" and "Would you like a cocktail?" Some restaurant managers like you to announce your name and that you will be the server for the meal. You may want to inform the guests of unlisted specials at this time. After a few minutes, ask, "May I take your order?" If you seated them, approach them again with a pleasant "Are you ready to order now?"

The host or hostess of a party may wish to order for his or her guests. The host or hostess is the spokesperson and will address the server for the entire group. He or she is the person most attentive to the welfare of all the members of the party and often takes the seat at the head of the table. Approach the host or hostess first from the left, and if he or she does not wish to order for the others, begin taking the order from the next person to the right.

If you are busy with another table when the newest party of guests is seated in your station, approach the new group and tell them you will be with them shortly. They will appreciate your attention and will not feel ignored.

TAKING ORDERS

TECHNIQUE OF TAKING ORDERS

Stand erect to the left of the guest with the order pad supported in the palm of your hand and a sharp pencil ready (Figure 4–2). Never place your book or order pad on the table to take an order. Use one of two techniques of taking the order that will help you identify the first person who orders and where to start serving when you bring the food:

1. Make a mental note of the first person who orders. If you are taking the order on paper rather than on the guest check, you may write down a unique characteristic identifying the first person. For example, note hair color, glasses, clothing, or tie. Then from that reference person, proceed taking orders counterclockwise around the table. When you serve the meal, you can serve exactly what each guest ordered without asking questions.

Figure 4–2   When taking the order, the waiter or waitress stands to the left of the guest and holds the order pad in the palm of the hand. Using a sharp pencil makes orders easy to read.

2. Note and circle the seat number of the first person who orders. Seat numbers should be understood in advance. For example, the seat on the kitchen side of the table can be known as seat number one, the seat to the left of this seat going counterclockwise is seat number two, and so forth. If all servers use this system, any other server or restaurant employee can deliver food to your table when you are busy.

Write clearly and systematically for your own benefit and that of the kitchen staff who must prepare the order exactly according to your instructions (Figure 4–3). Take the order completely. A few of the many questions you may have to ask the guests are as follows:

- Whether drinks should be iced
- Choice of salad dressing
- Choice of vegetable
- How meat should be cooked
- Sour cream or butter on baked potatoes
- How eggs should be cooked
- When to serve coffee

Use common abbreviations known to kitchen staff when you take orders. Some common abbreviations are shown in Figure 4–4. To prevent error, you may repeat the order back to the guests for their confirmation, especially when the order is given in an irregular fashion. Collect the menu from each guest after you write his or her order.

METHODS OF TAKING ORDERS

There are three main methods of taking orders in restaurants:

1. **A checklist system.** The waiter or waitress simply checks off the designated selection on a preprinted list of menu items (Figure 4–5). This method is used in short-order, fast-food establishments that have a limited a la carte menu.

2. **A guest-written order.** The waiter or waitress supplies each guest with a pencil and order blank, and the guest writes down his or her selection. The server then collects the orders and takes them to the kitchen. This method is rarely used but may be found in some more exclusive restaurants that serve elaborate luncheons.

3. **A waiter- or waitress-written order.** This method is most commonly used in large dining rooms. It gives the most satisfying results in restaurants whose menus have table d'hôte listings with several parts of each guest's meal to be noted.

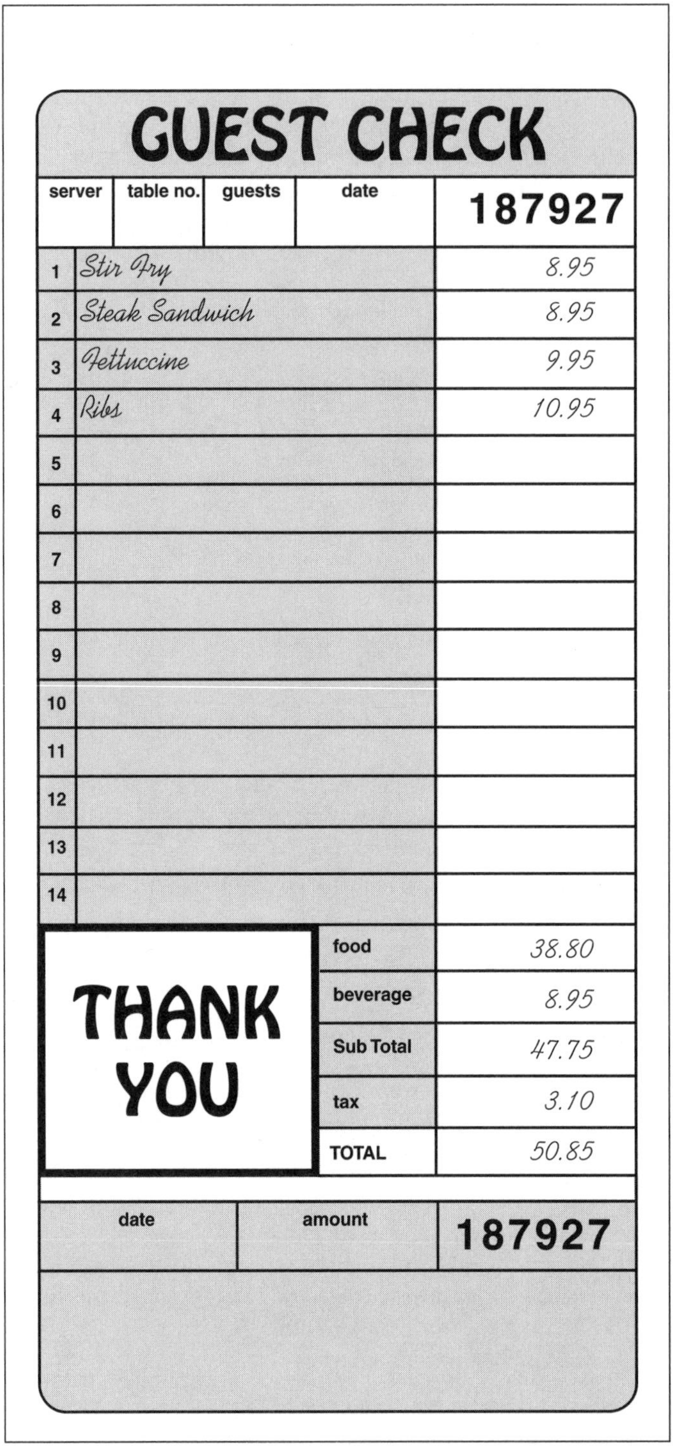

GUEST CHECK

server	table no.	guests	date	187927

1	Stir Fry	8.95
2	Steak Sandwich	8.95
3	Fettuccine	9.95
4	Ribs	10.95
5		
6		
7		
8		
9		
10		
11		
12		
13		
14		

THANK YOU	food	38.80
	beverage	8.95
	Sub Total	47.75
	tax	3.10
	TOTAL	50.85

date	amount	187927

Figure 4–3 The server should always write the order neatly and legibly on the guest check to ensure that it is read out correctly.

beverage

1	*3 tap beer*	*5.85*
2	*1 wine cooler*	*3.10*
3		
4		
5		
6		
7		
8		
9		
10		
11		
12		
13		
14		
TRANSFER TO FRONT	**TOTAL**	*8.95*

THANK YOU

This receipt is for your convenience

guests names   firm

Figure 4–3   (con't)

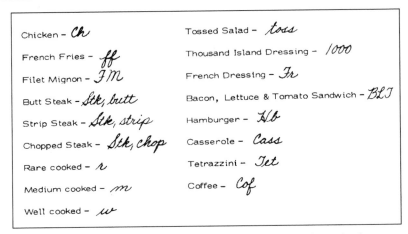

Figure 4–4   Menu abbreviations like these should be agreed upon for use by the servers and kitchen staff. Using them speeds up writing the order.

Servers can write orders in either of two main ways as follows:

1. **The order may be taken directly on guest checks**. The bar order is recorded on the back and the food order is recorded on the front of the check (Figure 4–3), or the bar order may be taken on a separate check. The food check is placed on a rotating wheel or other device in the kitchen and filled by the chef in turn with other orders. It is returned to you when you pick up the meal from the kitchen. Then the bar total is added to the food total and the check is presented to the guest for payment.

   Taking the order directly on the guest check is most satisfactory when the menu is printed with numbered meal combinations such as breakfasts and luncheons. To use this type of method, the kitchen should be a single unit so that the check is not excessively handled.

2. **The selections may be noted on a pad of paper**. Carbon copies are made or parts of the order are then rewritten for the kitchen staff, and the original order is retained by the waiter or waitress, who uses it to serve cocktails, appetizers, salads, and other items. After the meal, the waiter or waitress summarizes the order on a guest check and presents the check to the guest for payment.

   This way of taking the order is advantageous when the menu contains principally table d'hôte selections and the waiter and waitress are responsible for dishing up some courses, such as soups, salads, and desserts, and serving them in the proper order. This way of taking the order is also used with a multiunit kitchen consisting of a separate area and chef for steam table food (stews, soups), grilled foods (eggs, steaks, chops), and cold foods (salads, appetizers).

Steer Restaurant

730 CLIFTY DR.   MADISON, INDIANA 47250
812-273-4386

SERVER	STATION			CHECK NO..
				119953

Qty	Item							Amount
1	BIG STEER	PLATTER	P	(L)	S	C		2.25
	HAMBURGER	PLATTER	P	L	S			
	CHEESEBURGER	PLATTER	P	L	S			
1	FISH SAND.	PLATTER	P	(L)	S			2.45
	TEXAN	PLATTER				O		
	DANDY BOY	PLATTER		L	S	T		
	BREADED TENDERLOIN	PLATTER		L	S	T		
	GRILLED CHEESE	PLATTER						
	CHARBURGER	PLATTER				O		
	BLT SANDWICH	PLATTER		L	M	T		
	BLT CLUB	PLATTER		L	M	T		
	TUNA SALAD	PLATTER		L	M			
	GRILLED CHICKEN	PLATTER		L	M	T		
	FISHTAIL SANDWICH	PLATTER		L	S			
	GRILLED TENDERLOIN	PLATTER						

CHICKEN	SEAFOOD COMBINATION
SPAGHETTI	HAM STEAK
FISH DINNER	PORK CHOPS
BROILED FISH DINNER	CHICKEN STRIPS
SHRIMP DINNER	BROILED CHICKEN
CHICKEN FRIED STEAK	

C.B. GROUND BEEF STEAK	10 OZ. STRIP SIRLOIN
COUNTRY FRIED STEAK	12 OZ. T-BONE
6 OZ. RIBEYE	PRIME RIB
8 OZ. RIBEYE	PORK SPARE RIBS

OE O OM OW H SCH	HAM BAC SAU STK	
1	*choc. sundae*	1.95
1	*cherry pie*	1.65

CHEESE	H&C	WEST	SPAN	SUPREME
HOT CAKE 1-2-3	B&G			

SALAD BAR					
TOSSED SALAD	BC	TI	FR	RA	OV
SLAW	COTTAGE CHEESE		APPLESAUCE		
CHEF SALAD		LG	SM	SUPREME	LG
FF		ONION RING		B.P.	

Qty						Amount
2	(COLA)	DIET	(SPRITE)	ROOT B.	COFFEE	1.70
	MILK	LEMONADE	TEA	C-MILK	HOT CHOC	

THANK YOU PLEASE COME AGAIN

Figure 4–5 A waiter or waitress needs to indicate only the quantity or size of each item selected and extend the amount of the charge on a checklist order like this.

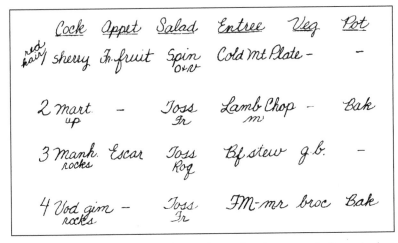

Figure 4–6   A waiter or waitress written order may be taken on a pad of paper in chart form as shown here.

A chart is made on a blank order pad with headings for each course or food selection. Guests are identified down the left margin and their choices noted under the appropriate headings (Figure 4–6). A glance at a column quickly indicates the entire party's choice of salads or entrées.

APPROPRIATE TOPICS OF CONVERSATION

Brief conversation with guests, or small talk, is a pleasant part of your job and makes the guests comfortable in restaurant surroundings. Keep comments and topics positive in nature; you can always find something nice to say. Small talk may include complimentary comments about menu items, food suggestions, and opinions about the weather. Avoid any negative comments such as those that may concern coworkers or the restaurant owners and the specifics of problems in the kitchen. Also resist the temptation to discuss your personal life or that of the customer. Keep small talk short and pleasant while attending to your work as waiter or waitress. If guests are busy talking among themselves, attend to your business of serving without entering into the conversation.

ANSWERING QUESTIONS

As a waiter or waitress, you are asked questions about food, the restaurant, the community, and even the state. Prepare yourself to answer questions by reading and listening. Be knowledgeable enough to answer questions intelligently and "suggestion sell" (discussed in the next section). You should know the following information about your restaurant:

- The hours and the address of the restaurant
- The menu and the ingredients in every dish served. Know the special of the day. Also know the general menu of other dining rooms and coffee shops on the premises and the hours they are open
- Historic facts of interest about your restaurant and community
- Events and attractions in the community, area, and state

If you are asked a reasonable question that you cannot answer, find out from someone who knows. For example, when a guest asks if there are onions in the beef bourgignonne and you do not know, say, "I don't know, but I'll ask the chef."

Many restaurants have a staff meeting about 11:00 A.M. or 4:00 P.M. so the hostess or maître d'hôtel can go over the menu for the day and announce changes in service. At this meeting, you are informed of the specials, soup selection, and dessert assortment, and about large groups that have reservations. In other restaurants, food and service changes are posted for you to read when you come to work.

▓▓▓▓ MAKING SUGGESTIONS

Making suggestions in a restaurant means to recommend foods, beverages, and services to make the meal more enjoyable for the guests; happy guests become regular patrons. Making suggestions also benefits you and the restaurant because you can increase the size of the guest check and consequently the size of the tip.

Suggest cocktails before the meal and perhaps cold or hot appetizers to enjoy with cocktails. Suggest side orders that complement the entrée, such as ham with omelets and mushrooms with steak. Also suggest beverages, desserts, and afterdinner cordials. Suggesting foods from seafood and salad bars and dessert tables is particularly advisable because the mouth-watering displays of foods should almost sell themselves. Some dessert displays are on trays or mobile carts that can be wheeled directly to the guest's tables for presentation.

During a special training session or periodic sessions in conjunction with menu changes, the manager or trainer may actually let you taste the foods served in the restaurant. This is a wonderful way to become acquainted with foods so you can answer any questions and make recommendations. When asked to help a guest choose between two menu selections say why you would recommend one. Do not degrade the second choice. Another way of helping a guest select is to describe preparation and accompaniments of each thus letting the guest decide from the additional information.

Figure 4–7 Whet the appetite of the customer by suggesting specific foods such as this white chocolate torte.

When you suspect that customers are budgeting, suggest the inexpensive special. For those who are celebrating, suggest the wine list or a birthday dessert or cake if your restaurant offers one. Another service is to suggest bringing an extra plate to divide a regular portion between children or to suggest children's portions or menus.

Avoid being overbearing or pushy about suggesting foods and beverages. Suggest only in a helpful way, and be sure your suggestions are appropriate to the meal. Be specific when you suggest a food. "Will there be anything else?" and "Would you like dessert?" are too general. Ask specifically if the guests would like the schaum torte or the apple pie a la mode. When they ask you what is good today, reply with a specific suggestion instead of saying, "Everything is good."

As you master the art of making specific suggestions, you can whet the appetite of the guests by appropriate adjectives that tempt the palate. For instance, say, "Would you like to begin your meal with a chilled appetizer of fresh New England shrimp?" or "May I suggest our cherries jubilee?" Or you might have an opportunity to describe a food item in appetizing terms such as "Our beef bourgignonne is made from cubes of choice sirloin simmered in a delicious blend of onions and burgundy" (Figure 4–7).

▮▮▮ TIMING THE MEAL

The server has the responsibility to time the entire meal so the guest's pace is methodical and comfortable, but neither rushed nor delayed. You are the sole communication link between the guests and the kitchen. If guests indicate they are in a hurry, guide them to menu items that can be prepared quickly instead of rushing the chef.

After taking the complete order, the waiter or waitress must decide when to place it in the kitchen. A good rule of thumb is to submit the entrée order just prior to serving the appetizer. Hold the order for a short time when you see the guests are lingering over cocktails.

In a single-unit kitchen, the chef sees that the entire order is ready at the same time. The only responsibility of the server is to submit the order as soon as possible. In a multiunit kitchen, the server coordinates the meal and submits the order in accordance with the length of time necessary to prepare the entrées. The meal order may have some entrées that take more preparation time than others (see the section on Preparation Times in Chapter 3). Submit these orders in separate stages so that they are ready at approximately the same time. For example, knowing that pork chops and a medium steak take 15 minutes, a chef's salad takes ten minutes, and beef burgundy is ready immediately, submit the grill order first, the salad order five minutes later, and the steam table order last. By placing the orders in this fashion, they are ready simultaneously, assuring that hot foods are hot and cold foods are cold. Dessert orders should be submitted and picked up immediately after the meal.

■■■■ PLACING ORDERS
IN THE KITCHEN

The method of communicating the orders to the kitchen staff varies among restaurants depending upon their size, type of kitchen, type of service, and availability of a computer system. There are three main ways of communicating the orders to the kitchen:

1. In some restaurants, you orally communicate the order to the kitchen by entering the kitchen and clearly giving the order to the proper chef, who may write down the order.

2. In some restaurants the order may be written on a guest check and given to the chef, who can arrange all the orders in sequence. The chef may attach them to a rotating wheel, spindle, or clip device so that your order will be filled in its turn (Figure 4–8). Occasionally in larger kitchens, waiters and waitresses must rewrite parts of the order for the separate kitchen units, as described previously. Separate department orders are shown in Figure 4–9.

3. In other restaurants the order is keyed into a computer terminal and sent to the chef electronically (see the section in Chapter 7 on Getting Orders To and From the Bar and Kitchen).

Some waiters and waitresses put orders back in their jacket or apron pockets and actually forget about them. Regardless of the system you use, chefs do not prepare orders until they receive them.

Figure 4–8 In many restaurants food orders are attached to a rotating wheel and then filled by the chef in turn.

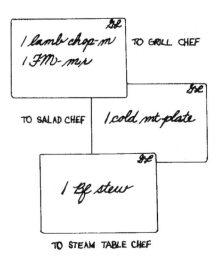

Figure 4–9 In some restaurants waiters and waitresses have to rewrite parts of the order for the various food preparation departments in the kitchen.

Figure 4–10   One of the several ways in which the waiter or waitress is notified that the order is ready is by lights on a clock. A lighted number signals a specific server to pick up an order in the kitchen.

████ PICKING UP ORDERS FROM THE KITCHEN

You may be notified in various ways that your order is ready to be picked up from the kitchen. A lighted number on the wall of the dining room may indicate your order is ready (Figure 4–10), or the chef may take the responsibility of orally notifying you. Some waiters and waitresses wear an electronic device that signals them by beeping or vibrating when their order is ready.

Compare the food with the order to see that the order is complete. Be sure the food is attractively arranged and garnished. Remedy any of your mistakes or those of the chef at this time. Arrange the plates on the tray so that they are well balanced to carry to the table.

 ## QUESTIONS

1. What restaurant personnel are responsible for seating the guests?
2. What determines the smoking policy in a restaurant?
3. Why is seating the guests advantageous instead of allowing them to seat themselves?

4. What are some of the clues that may help you identify the host or hostess of a party of guests?

5. Describe one or more methods to help you remember the items each guest ordered.

6. Why is the waiter- or waitress-written order on a pad of paper most popular for dining rooms with table d'hôte selections on the menus?

7. Why do order methods differ from one restaurant to another?

8. What are some topics that are appropriate for conversation with guests?

9. What suggestions would you make in the following instances?

   a. A guest orders apple pie

   b. The guests have finished their dessert

   c. A couple is celebrating their anniversary

10. Suggest the following in appetite-whetting terms:

    a. Antipasto

    b. Monte Cristo sandwich

    c. Lasagne

    d. Salmon fillet

    e. Baked Alaska

11. Explain the procedure for timing the following entrée meal order in a restaurant with a multiunit kitchen: chateaubriand; red snapper; lamb chops; pork chops; and shrimp soufflé.

 PROJECTS

1. Role-play seating the guests. Include conversation with the guests, placement of parties in the dining room, removal of extra serviceware, provision of water, and other services to make the guest comfortable.

2. Meet with service and kitchen personnel and agree upon abbreviations for food items on the menu. Make a list and post them in the kitchen. Or, as a trainee group, make a list of common abbreviations from a menu. Discuss the necessity of uniform use of abbreviations by all personnel.

3. Practice taking orders from fellow trainees posing as guests. Be sure to include suggestion-selling.

4. Describe the method of order taking used in your restaurant. Or, as a trainee group, select a familiar restaurant and discuss its ordertaking methods.

5. Investigate community events and attractions that would interest your guests. Get information from the city hall, chamber of commerce, service clubs, newspapers, radio publicity, and historical societies.

6. Go to restaurants of various sizes and types and ask service personnel how they place and pick up orders in the kitchen. Bring the information to class and discuss it with other trainees.

SERVING
THE MEAL

Serving means bringing the food and beverage order to the table and attending to the guest's needs throughout the meal. Good service involves serving foods and beverages in an efficient manner that combines proper serving techniques and courteous attention to the guests. It also means being prepared to handle unusual circumstances during the course of service. Finally, serving includes the suitable handling of the payment and tip.

■■■■ SERVING TABLES AND BOOTHS

SERVING EACH COURSE

Women and elderly people are served first out of traditional courtesy unless the party consists of a host or hostess entertaining friends. In that case, begin with the guest of honor at the host's or hostess's right. Continue serving around the table counterclockwise. If you have taken the order correctly you will never have to ask the guest what he or she has ordered as you serve.

Serve all foods, such as appetizers, soups, salads, entrées, and desserts, from the left of the guest with your left hand (Figure 5–1). Support the dish with your fingers underneath the plate and your thumb on the rim, and place it in the center of the cover. Using your left hand may take practice if

Figure 5–1   All foods should be served from the left of the guest, and dishes should be placed with the server's left hand.

you are right-handed, but the left-handed serve eliminates the possibility of elbowing the customer.

Each course is served as follows:

1. The course that is usually served first is the appetizer. The appetizer is a food item served before the meal, such as shrimp cocktail, oysters on the half shell, fruit, or juice. In a traditional restaurant this first course is placed on a small plate called an *underliner* and centered before the guest. A seafood fork is brought with the shrimp cocktail and oysters. It is either placed on the right-hand edge of the underliner or inverted into the bowl of the outside spoon of the table setting. In less formal restaurants appetizers like chicken fingers or nachos may be served in special divided dishes and may or may not be served on an underliner.

2. Soup may be served in place of the appetizer or as a second course. It is served in a small, handleless cup on a saucer. A soup spoon must be provided if it is not furnished with the table setting. Serve the soup in the center of the cover with the soup spoon on the right side of the saucer.

3. The salad is the next food served. It is placed to the left of the cover, allowing space in the center for the entrée. Salad dressing may be served in several ways. It may be brought to the table in a self-serve container, added to the salads in the kitchen according to the order, or served in small, individual containers on the side as requested by the guest. Black, fresh-ground pepper may be brought to the table in a

pepper mill and, if the guest agrees, added to the salad from the guest's left.

4. The entrée is the main part of the meal. First, be sure the table is properly set for the entrée selected. For example, with steak, add a steak knife, and with lobster, add lobster crackers and a seafood fork. Dinner rolls may be served with the salad course or, at this time, as an accompaniment to the entrée. Condiments such as steak sauce should be brought to the table when requested. Serve the entrée in the center of the cover. When serving a meat entrée, place any fatty part or bone away from the guest to ensure that the first bite will be pleasing. Next refill the water glasses.

5. The dessert is the last course served. A dessert fork or spoon should be brought with the food item and placed to the right of the dessert plate. Replenish coffee and water at this time. The service is complete when the guests ask for or you bring their check.

SERVING BEVERAGES

Give beverage service maximum attention throughout the meal. Take the cocktail order first, before the appetizer order. Table wines are opened and served when ordered (see Chapter 8, Wine and Bar Service), as are all other beverages. Keep glasses refilled with ice water, coffee cups filled with coffee, and wine glasses filled with wine until the bottle is empty. Suggest an after dinner drink when you take the dessert order.

Serve all beverages such as water, milk, coffee, and alcoholic beverages from the right of the guest with your right hand (Figure 5–2). Place beverages such as milk or tea to the right of the cover, and refill beverages such as coffee or wine without lifting the cup or glass from the table. Whenever pouring a hot beverage for guests seated close together, use a clean, folded napkin in your left hand and shield the guest from the hot container.

SERVING AT BOOTHS

By standing at the end of the booth, serve the guest farthest from you first with the hand farthest from the guest's seat. This means the guests on your right would be served their food with your left hand; the guests on your left would be served with your right hand. Serving in this manner prevents contact with the customer (Figure 5–3). However, always serve at the convenience of the guest, even if you must break the rules of proper service. For example, you may have to pick up the cup and pour coffee for a guest seated in a booth when serving properly is awkward.

CLEARING DISHES FROM THE TABLE

Clear the dishes when all guests at the table have finished the course. Often you can tell they are finished because the fork and knife are placed parallel

Figure 5–2 When pouring beverages, the server should leave the glass or cup on the table and pour with the right hand from the right of the guest.

to each other on the plate. When in doubt, ask if they are finished. Then remove all soiled dishes and utensils completely before serving the next food item. Clear dishes from the right of the guests with the right hand. Again, move from guest to guest in a counterclockwise direction around the table. In addition to dishes, pick up all cracker wrappers and soiled silver.

Clear soiled dishes to a nearby tray on a tray stand. Work quietly and efficiently, and never scrape or stack the dishes at the table. Stack the dishes on the tray so they are well balanced and safe for you to carry to the kitchen (see the section on Safety: Preventing Accidents in Chapter 6).

Before dessert, you should remove all dishes except water glasses and coffee cups, and crumb the table. Crumbing the table is the process of sweeping loose food particles into a clean plate to make the table more presentable. This can be done with a clean, folded napkin or with a *crumber*, a pencil-length metal tool with a groove in it for sweeping the table clean.

▮▮▮ EFFICIENCY WHEN SERVING

MINIMIZING STEPS

Time is important when serving guests, and you can save time by minimizing steps whenever possible. Never walk back to the kitchen empty-handed.

Figure 5-3 When serving guests seated in booths, serve each guest with the hand farthest from the guest: serve guests at the server's right with the left hand; serve guests at the left with the right hand.

Take dirty dishes back to the kitchen on your way to pick up food. You then have a tray stand available when you come out with your order.

By cutting down your time spent serving guests, you not only increase the number of people you can serve but also increase your efficiency. An increase in the number of guests served and faster service increases your tips.

MAINTAINING FOOD QUALITY

Serve hot foods hot and cold foods cold. Pick up and serve foods in the order that will maintain this temperature quality. For example, when serving several tables, pick up salads and crackers first and hot soups or cold ice cream last on the same tray. Likewise, serve the hot soup or cold ice cream first and the salad and crackers last.

ATTENDING TO GUESTS

There is no excuse for ignoring the guest. Allow little delay between courses and keep your eye on the guests as you serve others in your station. Guests indicate they need you by a look, gesture, or remark, and you should respond promptly to their needs.

Special attention should be given after you have served the entrée. When the guests begin to eat the main course, check back to be sure that all entrées are as ordered, satisfactory, and complete. Mistakes can be remedied easily at this time, and the guest is not angry or dissatisfied. The end of a meal is too late to adjust a complaint. Replenish rolls, water, and coffee quietly. Give guests an appropriate amount of attention. Beware of giving too much attention by hovering over guests, monopolizing the conversation, and constantly interrupting.

GIVING SPECIAL AMENITIES

Often customers will want to take home food on their plates that they were unable to finish eating. The restaurant will provide plastic bags, styrofoam boxes, or some other type of container for this purpose. Remove the guest's plate to a sidestand or kitchen and box the uneaten portion for the guest.

Another service is to present a mint to each guest at the table when you bring the check. Some restaurants may instead present a free biscotti, fortune cookie, after dinner wine, chocolate, or some other form of appreciation for the guest's patronage.

Many restuarants give a free dessert to patrons who have a birthday or anniversary. Servers may even gather around the guest(s) of honor and sing an appropriate celebration song.

▮▮▮ HANDLING UNUSUAL CIRCUMSTANCES

YOUR BEHAVIOR TOWARD ALL GUESTS

A good waiter or waitress strives to serve all guests equally well. Thousands of satisfied customers are necessary to run a restaurant successfully, and a server cannot be particular about which customers he or she serves. Most guests appreciate your efforts but some are difficult to please. Handle each situation, no matter how unusual or unpleasant, with genuine interest in serving the guest the best way you know how.

HANDLING GUESTS WITH SPECIAL NEEDS

Occasionally, servers encounter customers who have special needs, such as guests who are very young, disabled, or intoxicated.

Very Young Guests. If your assigned party of guests includes a young child, suggest a highchair or booster seat, if appropriate. Place the highchair at the table out of the aisle. Do not attempt to secure the child in the highchair or booster seat yourself. It is the parent's responsibility to be sure the child is secured so that the child will not fall out and sustain an injury. Treat the child as an important person. Be patient and pleasant, and assist the parents in making the child comfortable. Without being obvious, move the sugar, salt, pepper, and breakable items out of the child's reach.

Some restaurants have children's menus; however, never take a child's order without consulting the parents. Do not fill glasses too full. Use low

Figure 5–4 When dining out with children, parents appreciate favors or activities, such as crayons and paper, that will keep children occupied while they wait for their meals.

dessert dishes and tumblers instead of stemmed glassware. Parents appreciate extra napkins, bibs, crackers, novelty placemats, and favors for their children (Figure 5–4). Cheerfully warm an infant's bottle when asked, but return it warmed to the parent, not child, so the parent can test it for a safe temperature. If children are playing in the aisles or disturbing other guests, suggest to the parents that they keep them at the table to prevent injury to the child.

Disabled Guests.   Occasionally, a person who is disabled comes into a restaurant alone. Be attentive to his or her needs. The guest will tell you how he would like to be helped. Understanding the disability and assisting him or her properly and discreetly helps the guest enjoy the meal. For example:

- A person in a wheelchair may wish to be pushed up to the table, but be sure the wheelchair is out of the aisle. This guest may need assistance with the salad bar.

- A person who is visually disabled needs a lot of attention, but be careful not to be offensively oversolicitous. Hang up the guest's coat and belongings and gently lead the guest to a seat. Discreetly move objects to the areas he or she requests. Quietly ask if you may acquaint the guest with the menu. Then let the guest select the meal—the guest will select easily handled items. Assist the guest with the salad bar. Do not fill glasses too full. As you serve, inform the guest where the food and beverage items are being placed and whether or not the plate itself is hot.

- A person who is hearing impaired may be able to give you an order verbally like any other guest. Some, however, prefer to write out or point to their choices. Be alert to the fact that people who are hearing impaired speak with hand movements. If you are concerned about an accident, gently touch the person on the right or left shoulder indicating you are serving from that side.

Intoxicated Guests. Guests who are intoxicated should be seated in the back of the dining area or in a private dining room where they do not disturb other diners. Sometimes a guest who is intoxicated is bothersome or rude. Under no circumstances should you serve an intoxicated guest more alcohol in your establishment (see Chapter 8, Wine and Bar Service). Suggest nonalcoholic drinks or coffee. Be tolerant and call the manager if the situation goes beyond your control. Be sure the guest remembers to pay the bill.

HANDLING COMPLAINTS

Complaints arise when guests do not get the food and service they feel they deserve. In general, the better the table service and food quality, the fewer the complaints. Do not take offense, however, when guests do complain. Valid complaints are the restaurant's feedback and should be used to improve service for those who come to the restaurant in the future. Allowing a complaint to be ignored or handled poorly will result in a disgruntled guest. A disgruntled guest will spread negative word-of-mouth advertising about the restaurant.

Some complaints can be prevented before they occur. For example, if a guest orders a separate side order for which there is a charge, mention the extra charge for this specialty so they are not surprised when they find it on their check. When the order is delayed in the kitchen, reassure the guest that the order has not been forgotten. Remain professional and never place blame on other employees for a mistake or a delay, especially when the table is under your control.

By all means, avoid arguing with customers. Use tact and courtesy, and respect their opinions. Remember, the customer is always right. A good procedure for handling complaints is as follows:

1. *Listen* to the details of the complaint.

2. *Restate* the complaint briefly to show you understand.

3. *Agree* truthfully to a minor point, for example, "You are right to bring that up." This puts you in the position of looking at the complaint from the guest's side.

4. *Handle* the complaint promptly. Make an immediate adjustment or correction if you can. Treat your customer as you would like to be treated if you were in that position.

Figure 5–5 When guests have finished their meal, bring the check. It may be presented on a tip tray or in a folding wallet, as seen here, from the left of the guest.

■■■■ THE GUEST CHECK AND PAYMENT

When the guests indicate they have finished, complete the check and present it to the left of the host. This may be done in one of two ways:

1. The check may be placed face down on the table. Thank the guest and make brief departure remarks like "You may pay the cashier" and "Come back again soon." The guest then pays the cashier (Figure 5–5).

2. The check may be presented face up on a tip tray or enclosed in a folding wallet and the host pays you. When the host pays you, take the tray or wallet, check, and payment to the cashier to complete the transaction. Return all change, on the tray (coins anchoring the bills) or in the wallet, to the table. Then thank the guests and invite them back again.

Today payment is often made by personal check or credit card instead of cash. Personal checks may be accepted for the amount of the guest check (plus any additional amount for tip the guest may wish to add). Read all parts of the check to be sure they are accurate and complete (Figure 5–6). Ask for acceptable identification such as a driver's license, and have the check authorized by your supervisor. Take precautions to avoid accepting a fraudulent check.

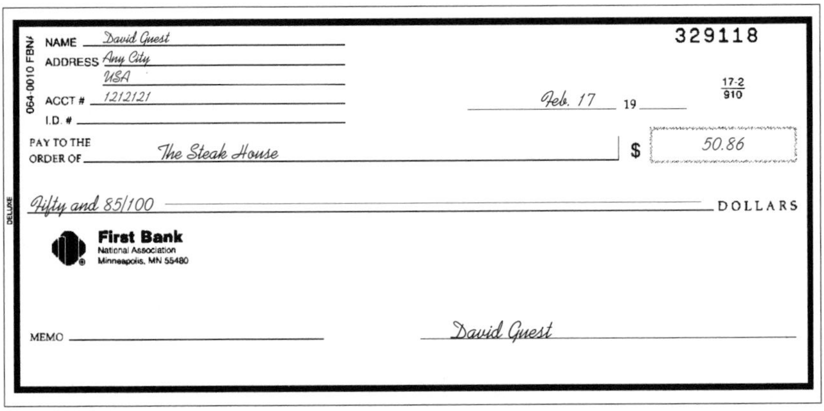

Figure 5–6   Examine all parts of a personal check carefully to make sure the date, restaurant name, both the numerical and written amounts, and the signature are correct. With practice, this can be done quickly.

Credit cards such as MasterCard, Diner's Club, American Express, Discover Card, and Visa are also used extensively in our mobile society. These cards should be signed by the cardholder. To use the card, place it in the addresser or stamping machine with the credit slip on top and slide the bar over both to imprint the slip, or print the credit slip with the computer printer. List dinners, tax, and bar total on the slip and total the amount (Figure 5–7). Adding on a tip is up to the cardholder. Bring a pen and have the guest check and sign the slip. Then compare the signature with the one on the credit card to be sure they are identical, and return the credit card.

■■■■ RECEIVING THE TIP

The tip or gratuity is a monetary reward for courteous and efficient service. Guests are not obligated to leave you any tip, but tipping is traditional. Tips are incentives to do a good job (Figure 5–8). If service is very good, the tip will usually be good. But sometimes tipping is based on the quality of food instead of the attention given by the server. Servers should remedy poor food quality with the kitchen so it does not reduce the size of the tip.

Tipping is very important because a server's base pay is low and tips make up the difference in earnings. Generally the size of the tip is between 10 and 20 percent of the total amount of the guest check. Although it is up to the discretion of the guest, the following is a well-accepted guideline for tipping:

- 10 percent for poor service
- 15 percent for average service
- 18–20 percent for good service
- over 20 percent for extraordinary service

A recent survey shows the average tip given in a restaurant is about 14 percent of the guest check total.

The tip may be given to you in various ways. If it is handed to you, thank the guest politely. If it is left on the table, pick it up before the table is cleared. If it is added to the charge slip by the guest or added automatically to the check by the restaurant, you will receive it from the cashier or on your paycheck.

If several servers share the responsibility of one table they should divide the tip. It may be the policy of the restaurant to have all servers pool their tips, then divide them equally at the end of the shift and share a percentage with the busboys and busgirls.

A good waiter or waitress should not worry about a regular customer who is pleased with service but does not tip well, or at all. Continue to give the steady customer your best service because regular customers can give the restaurant good recommendations and repeat business.

INCREASING THE TIP

There are many ways to increase the tip or be deserving of a generous tip. A few are listed below:

- Be neat in your appearance
- Give guests friendly greetings
- Be friendly and helpful, but be efficient
- Smile often when appropriate
- Check often to see if customers are in need of service, and offer to help them. You might say, "Is everything all right?" If it is not, take care of their needs
- Serve orders to customers as soon as possible
- Offer appropriate condiments with foods, such as steak sauce with steak, tartar sauce with fried fish, lemon with baked fish, and catsup with french fries
- Tell customers about specialties of the house. Use mouthwatering words to describe foods. Suggest appetizers, side orders, special beverages, and desserts that the guest may enjoy. This will increase the check, and with that, the tip (see the section in Chapter 4 on Making Suggestions)
- Pour water and coffee for customers as they need it
- When asked, give an appropriate number of one-dollar bills as change

REPORTING TIPS

Under federal law all tips count as taxable income. You must report all tips you receive to your restaurant manager and the Internal Revenue Service for paying income, social security, and Medicare taxes.

Servers earning $20 or more in tips in any one month must report the amount to their employer in writing. This includes tips earned in cash, on

Figure 5–7a Many types of credit cards are often used instead of cash to pay for a restaurant meal.

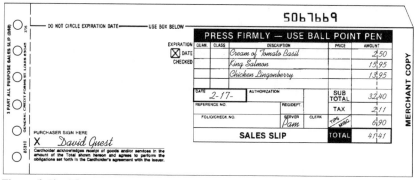

Figure 5–7b The card is imprinted on a sales slip like the one shown here.

credit cards, and those tips earned indirectly in tip pools. Fill out a report by the tenth day of the month following the month you earned the tips. Your report should include your name, address, and social security number, and the total tips you received during that period. Keeping a record of daily tips for yourself will be a good defense in proving the total tips earned in case of an audit.

Figure 5–7c Permission is granted from the credit card company by sliding the card through a machine that reads the number off the magnetic strip and authorizes its use.

Figure 5–8   The guest leaves a tip as a monetary reward for courteous and efficient service. Often the size of the tip depends upon how well the guest has been served

 QUESTIONS

1. Define *crumbing* and *appetizer*.
2. Briefly describe the differences between serving food and serving beverages.
3. What should you do if a guest asks you to take his plate before everyone at the table is finished with the course?
4. Why should you avoid scraping and stacking the dishes at the table in front of the guest?
5. How should you handle the complaint when the guest says:
   a. "The food is cold!"
   b. "My steak is too rare!"
   c. "The chili is too spicy!"
   d. "You spilled coffee on me!"
6. How can you protect a guest from the hot coffee pot when you are pouring coffee at the table?

7. Using the least number of coins and bills, indicate the amount of change to be returned for each of the following transactions:

   a. Given $5.00 for a $4.27 check

   b. Given $10.00 for a $7.56 check

   c. Given $15.00 for a $13.22 check

   d. Given $20.03 for a $12.78 check

8. Why is it true that you can increase your tips with fast, efficient service?

9. How should you react when a customer does not leave you a tip?

 PROJECTS

1. Role-play serving and clearing dishes from the table. Take turns being the guest and the waiter or waitress.

2. Observe waiters and waitresses when you are a guest in a restaurant, and note errors made by the service personnel. Discuss the points with other trainees.

3. Brainstorm ways to save time and effort in the serving process.

4. Discuss unusual circumstances concerning guests, other than those mentioned in this chapter.

5. Have one trainee learn and demonstrate the charge card transaction.

6. Interview a good server and find out what he or she would suggest to increase tips.

6

SAFETY, SANITATION, AND EMERGENCY PROCEDURES

Equally as important as knowing good serving techniques is using safe and sanitary work routines to protect yourself, your fellow employees, and guests while carrying out the duties of your job. Being prepared for a quick response in any emergency, such as a fire, tornado, or an electrical blackout, and knowing what to do for an injury or illness, is important to ensure that everything within reason is done for the safety and health of the guests.

▆▆ SAFETY: PREVENTING ACCIDENTS

Report to management any safety hazards that you see so that they can be corrected immediately. Develop a routine with other waiters and waitresses for a safe restaurant operation. Have on hand a well-stocked first-aid kit, including latex gloves, if an accident does happen. These are the joint responsibilities of everyone in the organization. Use the following suggestions to make your restaurant a safer place to work or visit:

1. Pass other workers on the right in the aisles between tables.

2. Look before pushing open a door so you do not bump into someone on the other side. Pull, do not push, carts through doorways.

3. Carefully follow manufacturer's instructions for mixing sanitizing solutions for wiping tables. Never mix cleaning materials.

4. Report or clean up any spilled food or beverage immediately. Put a chair over the spill while you get the proper supplies for cleaning it up. The most frequent customer mishaps in a restaurant are slips and falls.

5. Keep work and serving areas clean and orderly. Keep aisles clear at all times. Beware of tripping over purses or briefcases that may be in the aisle (Figure 6–1).

6. Keep exits clear and unlocked during operating hours for emergency evacuation.

7. Hot beverage temperature should be regulated in the kitchen so that beverages are hot but never scalding. To prevent guests from burning their mouths, pour hot beverages only when guests request refills or agree to a refill. If guests are seated close together shield the guest with a clean, folded towel or napkin as you pour a refill. Be sure the cup is on a table or tray when you pour hot beverages into it; never pour hot beverages while the guest is holding the cup.

Figure 6–1   Always check for briefcases, parcels, or purses that may have been placed on the floor because they can cause accidents.

Figure 6–2   Lift a heavy tray by bending your knees, keeping your back straight, and smoothly lifting the tray to shoulder height.

8. Stack dishes on trays so that they are well balanced. When picking up food in the kitchen, place full glasses in the center of the tray, and make sure handles and spouts are well within the edge of the tray. Soup bowls and coffee cups should be placed directly on the tray so they do not spill on the saucers. When clearing tables, never stack glasses one inside the other. Stack dishes only to a reasonable height to avoid the hazardous juggling act that so often results in breakage and injury.

9. Lift a stacked tray from a tray stand in the following manner: Stand close to the tray with your feet spread for balance. Bend your knees but keep your back straight and not twisted. Place your left hand (nonserving hand) under the center of the tray. Grasp the edge of the tray firmly with your other hand. Breathe in to inflate your lungs, then smoothly lift the tray to shoulder height (Figure 6–2). Bending your knees and lifting with your leg muscles prevents back strain.

10. Never lift trays of food or dirty dishes over the heads of customers.

11. Never pick up several glasses in one hand by inserting your fingers into the glasses. If you do break a glass, use a broom and dustpan or a damp paper towel or cloth, not your bare hands, to pick up the pieces.

12. If you do cut yourself or if anyone in the restaurant is injured or ill exposing others to blood or other body fluids, the body fluid spills must be handled with a procedure called *Universal Precautions*. Universal Precautions is a standard by which all blood (and other body fluid) is treated as if potentially infected with HIV (Human Immunod-

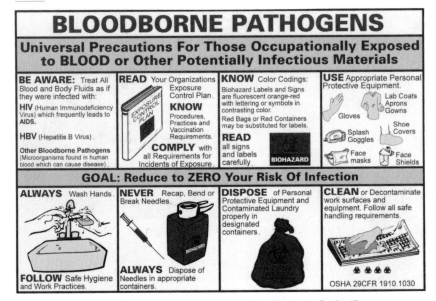

Figure 6–3   Universal Precautions are guidelines for handling body fluid spills to assure zero risk of infection to the server.

eficiency Virus) or HBV (Hepatitus B Virus). HIV and HBV are diseases which are untreatable. Universal Precautions are guidelines that detail cleaning up of potentially dangerous body fluids while wearing personal protective equipment such as gloves and other protective clothing, and decontaminating surfaces and disposing of stained rags to assure a zero risk of infection (Figure 6–3).

13. Wear shoes with low rubber heels to prevent slipping.
14. Let parents place and secure their child in a highchair or booster seat. The safety of the child is the responsibility of the parent.

███ SANITATION RESPONSIBILITIES

The U.S. Public Health Service Food Code Manual for 1993 states that foodborne illnesses in the United States are a major cause of personal distress, preventable death, and avoidable economic burden. Millions of people become ill from microorganisms in food resulting in an estimated 10,000 deaths each year. The annual cost of foodborne illness is estimated to be between $7.7 and $23 billion.

The Center for Disease Control and Prevention has stated that where reported foodborne outbreaks were caused by mishandling of food, most of the time the mishandling occurred within the retail segment of the food industry. This retail segment includes markets, schools, churches, camps, institutions, vending locations, and restaurants.

Since restaurant food is identified as part of the problem, every employee in the restaurant has the responsibility to improve sanitary eating conditions for guests. Improper food and utensil handling can lead to contamination and then foodborne illnesses, hurt the reputation of a restaurant, or close the restaurant permanently. Using the following suggestions can help to prevent food contamination in your restaurant:

1. Wear effective hair restraints if your hair is long to prevent hair from getting in the food or on food preparation surfaces.

2. Make sure your uniform, apron, hands, forearms, and fingernails are clean to avoid the transfer of harmful bacteria to the food.

3. Wash your hands before starting work, after using the restroom, eating, drinking, or smoking a cigarette, and as often as possible after clearing dirty dishes and handling money. A minimum of 30 seconds of good hand scrubbing with soap and thoroughly rinsing with clean water is necessary to remove soil and contamination.

4. Keep your hands away from your hair, scalp, and face. When you sneeze or cough, use a tissue and then wash your hands.

5. Do not work if you have an open wound, a cold, the flu, or any other communicable or infectious disease. Notify your supervisor so he or she can find a replacement. Cover any boil or infected wound with a dry, tightfitting, sanitary bandage.

6. Do not work if you have or have been exposed to *Escherichia coli (E. coli)*, *Salmonella typhi*, or *Shigella* until you have medical documentation that you are free of these illnesses.

7. Hepatitis A is a serious inflammation of the liver caused by the hepatitis A virus. Without thorough handwashing it is possible for an infected server to transmit hepatitis A to others via food. Do not work if you have or have been exposed to hepatitis A virus until you have medical documentation that you are free of this illness.

8. Handle clean dishes by the rims, glasses by their bases, and silver by the handles to avoid contamination of food or lip-contact surfaces (Figure 6–4).

9. Store tableware in a clean, dry place at least six inches above the floor and protected from flies, dust, splash, and other contaminants.

10. Wipe tables and counters with a cloth rinsed in a sanitizing solution. Do not use these wiping cloths for any other purpose.

11. Bring a clean utensil to replace one that has fallen on the floor.

12. Avoid unnecessary contact with the soiled surfaces of tableware or linens and cross-contamination with clean tableware.

13. Keep dirty dishes completely separate from foods to be served to prevent contamination. Clear one course completely, removing it on a tray, before you bring the next course on another tray.

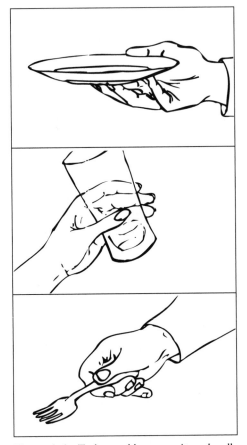

Figure 6–4 To keep tableware sanitary, handle dishes by the rims, glasses by their bases, and silver by the handles.

14. Pour refills without touching the rim of the glass or cup with the pitcher, wine bottle, or coffee server. This will prevent cross contamination from one guest's glass or cup to another.

15. Notify guests that clean plates are to be used each time they return to self-serve areas such as buffet and salad bars.

▮▮ EMERGENCY PROCEDURES

Restaurant staff may have to manage a crisis situation at some time during their employment. A staff can be mindful of safety, but cannot prevent all fires, storms, or electrical blackouts, nor predict when someone in the restaurant will become injured or seriously ill. To be prepared for any incident attend frequent meetings to review emergency procedures so they become second nature. The staff's main responsibility is to encourage everyone to remain calm, to control panic and confusion, to have a plan of action, and, hopefully, to prevent serious consequences. The following information may help in an emergency.

FIRE

Fire is an occupational hazard to any kitchen-based business, and fires occur in restaurants every year endangering people and causing millions of dollars in property damage. A serving staff that is conscientious about safely handling open flames when cooking and using candles, keeping electrical equipment in good repair, carefully disposing of the contents of ashtrays into fireproof containers, and monitoring their own smoking habits is taking the first step in fire prevention.

Because fires do occasionally occur despite staff precautions, be prepared to keep order and begin evacuation immediately. Alert the fire department either from the restaurant phone, if it can be done safely, or from an outside phone. Keep guests calm and get them out of the building quickly following posted evacuation routes. Have a plan to cover all exits to make sure customers and coworkers leave and do not re-enter the building. Reassemble at a preplanned gathering point outside and notify firefighters if anyone is missing.

TORNADOES

Tornadoes are frightening realities. We cannot predict when or where a severe storm, such as a tornado, will strike, but there are some precautions we can take to minimize danger to people and property.

Learn the warning signals used in your area—know the difference between a "watch" and a "warning." A *watch* means conditions are favorable for tornadoes to develop. Be alert to changes in the weather by having one member of the staff listen to a local radio station. Be prepared to act quickly in the event that you hear a tornado warning siren. A *tornado warning siren* means that a funnel has actually been sighted in your area. If one is issued help guests seek shelter immediately!

Warn guests to stay inside and not to take cover in cars in the parking lot. Guests and staff should seek shelter in basements or inside rooms away from large windows. Encourage everyone to lie low with hands covering the back of the head to reduce the possibility of neck injury. Stay sheltered until the storm is over.

ELECTRICAL BLACKOUTS

Electrical failure may be temporary or long-lasting. If it is temporary, patience is your primary response, but if the electrical failure continues over a period of time, guests may be sitting in darkness at their tables and will need some lighting to continue dining or to move about safely.

Some public buildings have emergency lighting that is triggered by an outage. If this is not the case, or if additional lighting is needed, distribute candles or battery-powered lights to tables as soon as possible to illuminate the restaurant.

INJURY OR SERIOUS ILLNESS

Remain calm if a guest is seriously injured or becomes ill. Remember, your immediate responsibility is to the welfare of the guest. Knowing first-aid techniques may be a valuable skill at this time. Know your state's "good Samaritan" laws which limit your liability if you help in a crisis situation.

It is advisable for the entire staff, or at least one person per shift, to be trained in first aid and personal safety so they can react correctly in an emergency. *First aid* is defined as treatment for minor injuries or help until more complete treatment by medical personnel can be provided. Trained servers should also know cardiopulmonary resuscitation (CPR) and the abdominal thrust maneuver (Heimlich maneuver). Skills should be reviewed each year so responses become automatic and techniques are updated. A first-aid kit and latex gloves for treatment of injuries involving body fluids should always be on-hand. Post the emergency phone number or 911 near all restaurant phones.

Never move a guest who has been injured or is seriously ill unless it is a life-threatening situation. Immediately enlist the help of the restaurant manager and other members of the serving team. Someone should be sent to call for medical help while others stay with the victim to comfort him or her and to start first aid, if necessary. Some of the serving team should relocate nearby guests to other tables as far away from the incident as possible.

If first aid is necessary, obtain the consent of the injured or ill person and explain what first-aid procedures will be done. Ask permission from a parent if a child is the victim. If the injured is unable to communicate, you may give first aid because the law assumes the person would consent. For less serious injuries or illnesses offer to call paramedics or a doctor but let the victim decide.

One server should document the incident for insurance and liability purposes. Get names and phone numbers of people who witnessed the incident and document what they saw happen.

A common incident in restaurants is a customer's choking on food such as a large piece of steak. The guest may turn blue, stop speaking, and indicate choking by grasping his or her throat. The guest may also collapse. You may have to check the mouth or throat for food. Any food must be removed immediately. This may be done by a simple procedure called the "abdominal thrust maneuver" (formerly called the Heimlich maneuver). Stand behind the victim and wrap your arms around the waist; place your fist thumb-side against the abdomen slightly above the navel but below the rib cage; grasp your fist with your other hand and press into the victim's abdomen with a quick upward thrust. Repeat several times if necessary to expel the food (Figure 6–5).

Be sure to watch the guest's belongings. Possessions such as purses, parcels, and coats should be kept in a safe place until the guest recovers.

Figure 6–5   An emergency tactic called the abdominal thrust maneuver (Heimlich Maneuver) should be performed to save the life of a choking victim. Exerting pressure to force the diaphragm upward compresses the air in the lungs and expels the object blocking the breathing passage.

For any emergency you have an excellent chance to retain the respect of customers or fare well in a lawsuit if you have been conscientious about preventing accidents and sensitive to people involved in injuries and other emergencies.

 QUESTIONS

1. Who is responsible for preventing accidents in a restaurant?
2. What is the safe way to pick up broken glass?
3. What does the term "Universal Precautions" refer to?
4. When should you wash your hands while on the job?
5. List five sanitation responsibilities that involve personal grooming or hygiene.
6. What does a tornado warning siren indicate?
7. List all of the things you should do in the first 15 minutes after a guest suddenly sustains an injury or suffers a serious illness.

 PROJECTS

1. Practice loading a tray safely with different combinations of tableware and foods.
2. Have a group discussion about ways to improve safety in a restaurant for the server and then for the guest.
3. Place your unwashed fingers in a dish of agar-agar. Keep the dish in a warm place and check it daily for bacterial growth.
4. Have a health officer discuss with the trainees the sanitation laws of your city, county, and state as they apply to serving. In particular, discuss the laws relating to communicable and infectious diseases.
5. Invite a firefighter to demonstrate different kinds of fire extinguishers and how to identify which fires to use them on.
6. Post your local rescue squad telephone number next to the restaurant phone. Invite a local doctor to come to your training session and discuss first aid in emergency situations. Practice the abdominal thrust maneuver.
7. Ask a doctor or the Red Cross to recommend the right size or a list of items to be stocked in a first-aid kit for a restaurant. Assemble the items and explain the purpose of each at a staff meeting.

7

HANDLING THE SERVICE WITH A COMPUTER SYSTEM

M any restaurants use point-of-sale computer technology to improve their serving systems. Because this is the trend today, you must be familiar with certain waiter and waitress duties to be performed on the computer.

This chapter provides current information about restaurant computers. It describes the usual point-of-sale computer hardware that you might find in a restaurant dining area, such as server terminals, visual displays, printers, cash drawers, change dispensers, and hand-held order terminals. Handling the service electronically is discussed, with emphasis on taking the order, getting the order to the bar and kitchen, completing each transaction, and closing at the end of the day. The advantages of a computer system are also explained.

▪▪▪ COMPUTERS IN RESTAURANTS

More than half of all smaller restaurants and nine out of ten restaurants with annual sales of $1 million or more reported using computers as an aid in their operations. A restaurant computer may be an electronic cash register stand-alone unit operated by a cashier or a point-of-sale computer system that links the dining room(s), bar, kitchen, and office and is operated in the serving area by the waiters and waitresses. With a few hours of instructions, servers can learn to operate the computer equipment and be capable of using it competently in approximately a week.

There is even a seating management program for the computer that helps a maître d'hôtel or hostess maximize guest counts and keep tables full. This system provides the greeter with the status of seated tables and the approximate time when each table will again be open for reseating. The guesswork is taken out of quoting waiting times when the dining room is full; customers appreciate being quoted a realistic wait time.

Many restaurant managers feel there are advantages to being computerized. They are in agreement that a computer system makes serving in a restaurant more efficient. But a computer system will never replace the server or change the personal service given by the waiter or waitress.

◼ COMPUTER HARDWARE USED BY WAITERS AND WAITRESSES

Computer hardware is a term for the physical components of a computer system that accept and process the information fed into them at the restaurant. Computer hardware in the restaurant can be divided into two categories: back office computer hardware operated by the manager and dining area point-of-sale computer hardware operated by the servers. The central processing unit that is responsible for controlling all processes done by the computer and the memory that stores information are two examples of back-office hardware. The following are examples of dining room computer hardware.

SERVER TERMINALS

Server terminals are point-of-sale machines with a touchscreen or keyboard (Figure 7–1). They are connected to a back office central processing unit and are used to enter information, such as date, number of guests at a table, and food and beverage orders, into the system. The central processing unit in the manager's office determines exactly what is done with this information by the way it is programmed. Server terminals may be placed at convenient locations in or near the dining room, at the cashier's station to replace the traditional cash register, and in the bar.

The server terminal may have a keyboard that is *preset*, that is, dedicates each key to a specific menu item (Figure 7–2). By touching the preset key for the menu item wanted, the description and price are instantly recalled from the system's memory. For expanded menu pricing, additional menu

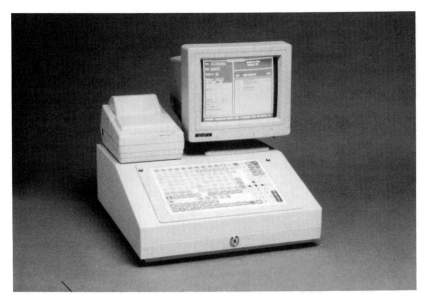

Figure 7-1 Waiters and waitresses use terminals to enter orders into the computer system. Terminals may have a display, printer, and preset keyboard as shown.

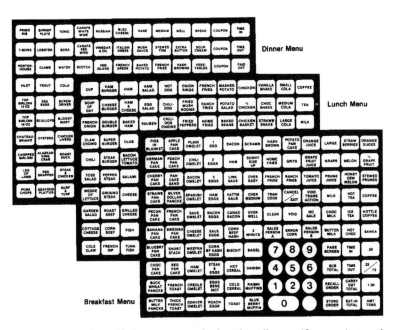

Figure 7-2 Each specific key on a preset keyboard recalls a specific menu item and price from the system's memory. This feature guarantees speed and accuracy when placing orders.

Figure 7–3   The server terminal may have a touch screen feature. The server merely touches the appropriate prompt on the screen to enter the order information.

items can be stored in the central processing unit and accessed by use of an automatic price look-up feature.

The server terminal may have a touch screen with prompts that guide the server through information input. The server merely touches the screen to enter the information. This eliminates the need for a keyboard (Figure 7–3). Server terminals may function by themselves or they may be equipped with other hardware attachments such as visual displays, printers, cash drawers, and change dispensers.

VISUAL DISPLAY

The visual display is a video screen that attaches to the server terminal. The items entered on the terminal keyboard by the server are projected line by line on the display. In this way the server can verify the information put into the terminal.

As another function of the display, step-by-step instructions may be programmed to appear on the screen to guide the server in using the terminal keyboard correctly. These instructions make using a computer terminal easy for servers.

A display may also be useful at cashier's stations or bars where management wants to have the guest see the items ordered or the amount owed. In dimly lit restaurants or bars, the lighting on the display can be adjusted so the words can be easily read.

Figure 7–4 A cash drawer below the server terminal makes this an electronic cash register.

PRINTERS

Printers are machines that imprint information on food and beverage orders, guest checks, receipts, and management reports. Menu items, quantity, preparation, meal accompaniments, and other information can be clearly described on paper. Printers are found in the bar and kitchen, at the cashier's station, and in the manager's office. The central processing unit is programmed to route items ordered by the server to the chef or bartender who can fill the order as it comes off the printer in the work area. Guest checks or tab receipts can be imprinted by the printer in the dining room or at a cashier's station. Management reports are stored for management use and are printed when they are accessed in the manager's office.

CASH DRAWER

A *cash drawer* is a drawer divided by denomination into money compartments and placed close to, or attached to, the terminal at a cashier's station. The addition of the drawer for making change, and perhaps a printer, converts the terminal to an electronic cash register and replaces the older model cash register (Figure 7–4).

CHANGE DISPENSER

An automatic change dispenser is a device that collects the right change from its coin reserve and distributes it to the customer (Figure 7–5). These are often found in fast-food restaurants attached to electronic cash regis-

Figure 7–5 A fast means of giving change to a customer at the cashier's station is by using a change dispenser. These are often found in casual or family-style restaurants.

ters. Change dispensers eliminate coin-handling errors and speed up guest settlement.

HANDHELD ORDER TERMINALS

A handheld order terminal is a small, portable, cordless computer terminal, with a keypad or touchscreen, used by servers to take orders from guests (Figure 7–6). It replaces the traditional order book or pad. The handheld order terminal is connected by radio transmission to larger terminals and printers so that orders placed on them are immediately sent to the bar and kitchen. A server can also check on orders or have immediate feedback on item availability or wine in stock. Handheld order terminals are not as common as stationary computer terminals but are recommended for busy bars, terraced dining rooms, alfresco dining, beach and poolside service, deck service on cruise ships, and dinner theaters with short intermissions for serving drinks.

TAKING ORDERS USING A COMPUTER SYSTEM

In most restaurants with a computer system, the server takes a guest's order on a traditional order pad or pad of paper. Having taken the complete

Figure 7–6 Some restaurant situations require a small, portable, handheld terminal that servers can use to take orders from the guests.

order, the waiter or waitress proceeds to a server terminal to open the guest's account and record the order in the computer.

Each server is given an identity key, a code number, or authorizing card that must be used to activate the server terminals in the dining room (Figure 7–7). The server then enters the identity key, number, or card to sign into the system. The waiter or waitress punches in the table number, number of guests in the party, and check number, and then inserts the guest check into the printer.

The server then keys in the order (Figure 7–8). Servers may either memorize a numbered listing of everything on the menu and push the correct numbers, or simply push a preset menu key on the terminal to enter the customer's menu choice into the system. Newer touch-screen terminals allow the server to record the order by touching the screen prompts. As food and beverage items are entered, they may be shown on the display for verification. Each entry contains quantity, description, accompaniments, preparation instructions, and price, and prints a guest check, the manager's journal, and a kitchen and/or bar order in one operation. The

Figure 7–7 Each server is given an identity key, code number, or authorizing card, as pictured. The card must be used to activate the server terminals in the dining room.

Figure 7–8 The server enters the order into the terminal in the dining room. This saves steps to the bar or kitchen to place the order.

system also automatically prints the date and time of the order on the guest check.

The server may easily add to the guest's order at a later time from the same terminal or a different terminal. This is possible because each guest check has a number and entering the number signs into the guest's account. Some numbers may also be in bar code, a code of lines representing that number, and can be "read" by the computer. When that number is read, the previous balance for that number is recalled from memory. As each additional menu item is punched into the terminal, it is sent to the kitchen or bar. The guest check is automatically positioned to the next available print line, and the new information prints on the guest check.

■■■■ GETTING ORDERS TO AND FROM THE BAR AND KITCHEN

Most restaurant computer systems have printers or displays in the bar and kitchen. As the server punches in the customer's order at the server terminal, the information is immediately transmitted to the appropriate remote order printer or display (Figure 7–9), and beverage and food orders are filled by the bartender and chef without delay (Figure 7–10).

A restaurant with only a single kitchen may have a computer function identifying cold food items in blue ink and hot food items in red ink on the same paper from the kitchen printer. In a restaurant with a multiunit kitchen, one printer can be placed at the hot foods production station and another in the cold foods section (Figure 7–11). The computer system may be programmed to split the order and send each specific menu item to the appropriate kitchen printer.

Following preparation, a person called an *expediter* may assemble complete orders and bring them to the dining room for the waiters and waitresses. This assistance helps facilitate efficient service and reduces kitchen traffic. In a restaurant without an expediter, the server is notified that the order is ready, picks it up from the kitchen, and serves the meal.

■■■■ COMPLETING EACH TRANSACTION

Some restaurants have a cashier's station and cashier to settle the guest's account. In other restaurants, the use of a computerized system has eliminated the need for this position because each server can do the work of a cashier. The computer records all items ordered, adds tax on taxable items, totals the guest check, and adds the gratuity, if policy. It can even split or combine checks, if requested by the guest.

At the end of the meal, the totaled guest check is presented to the guest for payment. When the guest has paid, the server takes the cash or credit

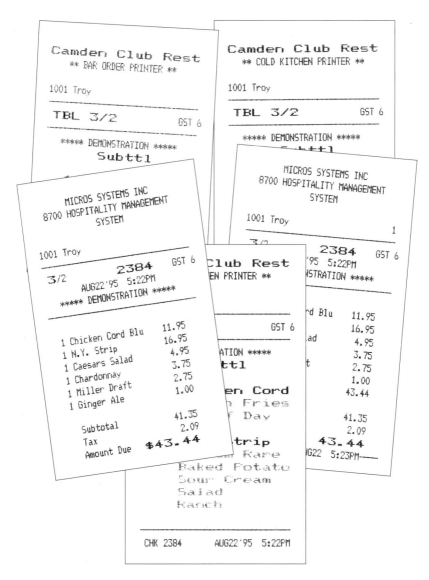

Figure 7–9 Each order placed in the computer system prints on a guest check and on various kitchen and bar printouts. The manager also has access to the order on the computer in the restaurant office.

card to a terminal and settles the check. The computer can act as the credit card authorization center.

The server must insert the guest check back into the terminal and validate each check total as proof of settlement (Figure 7–12). This applies regardless of whether the transaction is settled by cash or credit card. When settlement is completed, the guest's account is closed.

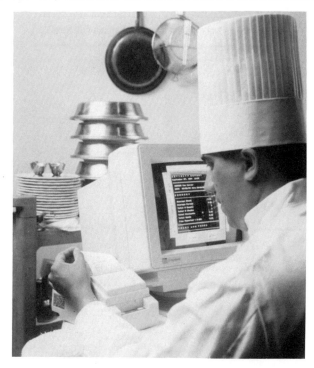

Figure 7–10 With a computer system, servers send clear, legible, timed orders to the chef in the kitchen, who fills them without delay.

■■■■ CLOSING AT THE END OF THE DAY

If the restaurant has a cashier's station, the cashier keeps all receipts of set-tlements and balances them at the end of the day. Otherwise, the server keeps money, checks, and credit slips collected as payment. As the waiter or waitress keys each order into the computer, the amount of the item is auto-matically and immediately charged to that server's account. The computer calculates all the drinks and menu items, puts in appropriate taxes, and totals the guest checks. At the end of the shift the server cashes out com-pletely, balancing the receipts in his or her pocket with guest check totals calculated by the computer.

■■■■ ADVANTAGES AND DISADVANTAGES OF A COMPUTER SYSTEM

Restaurants are using computer systems because they offer the following advantages to the serving staff:

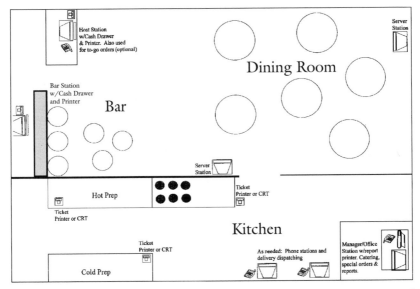

Figure 7–11   This diagram shows an example of a complete computer system. Server terminals are close to the dining room. Orders are automatically divided and channeled to the appropriate cold or hot preparation area, or bar, where chefs or bartenders fill a portion of the order.

1. **Save steps placing orders**. The average server walks ten to fifteen
   miles a day on the job. Most of the walking is done taking orders to and
   picking up orders from the kitchen and bar. With a restaurant computer, the order is sent electronically, which cuts down on the number of
   steps the servers must take to the bar and kitchen.

2. **Speed up service to the customer**. Placing orders electronically has-
   tens the flow of information to the bartender and chef. Orders can be
   filled quickly, which speeds up service to the customer, increases the
   number of customers who can be served, and pleases the customer with
   prompt service.

3. **Increase server productivity**. Because servers spend less time walking
   back and forth and handling guest checks, they have more time to
   spend with their customers. They have time to make suggestions about
   the menu, answer questions, and serve correctly. In restaurants with
   computer systems, the average customer's check increased by about ten
   percent, thereby increasing tips accordingly.

4. **Guarantee accurate food and beverage preparation**. With a computer system, waiters and waitresses send the bar and kitchen staff clear,
   legible, timed orders. There is no confusion over unusual abbreviations
   or illegible handwritten orders. The chef and bartender know which

Figure 7–12 To complete a transaction, the server must insert the guest check back into the terminal and press the key to total the check. This closes the account.

server ordered the food or drinks, the time the order was taken, what table that food was ordered for, the number of guests at the table, and exactly how the food or drinks are to be prepared.

5. **Eliminate confusion**. A hectic, fast-paced atmosphere is not always desirable in an elegant restaurant. Establishments with point-of-sale computer systems have less waiter and waitress traffic to the service bar and kitchen. A quieter, more relaxed mood can be maintained in the restaurant.

6. **Eliminate pricing errors on guest checks**. Restaurant computers automatically price menu items, wines, and drinks. Servers can also use a price look-up function. The computer does all the computations on the guest check, thereby eliminating errors in pricing, addition, tax calculation, discounts, and totals.

7. **Produce itemized guest checks at server stations**. Preprinted customer guest checks are not necessary because the computer has its own guest check form at the cashier's station or server terminal. The restaurant computer automatically produces clear, accurate, concise, itemized guest checks when the server needs to complete the guest's transaction. This feature eliminates the time-consuming delay as customers wait for servers to settle the guest check.

One disadvantage of a computer system is that timing a meal is difficult when entrées requiring different preparation times are placed in a multiunit kitchen. Some managers of restaurants like this have the server enter the order on the computer but place the order in the kitchen themselves. This system has no kitchen printers.

 QUESTIONS

1. What is the advantage of a computer seating management program over a conventional seating program?
2. Define *computer hardware.*
3. What are two examples of "back office" computer hardware in a restaurant?
4. What is a preset terminal keyboard and what is the advantage of this feature?
5. What is the advantage of the touch screen terminal over the keyboard system?
6. What types of information does the chef receive from the server on the kitchen printer?
7. Discuss the types of computer hardware that might be found at a cashier's station.
8. What are handheld order terminals and for what type of service situations might they be used?
9. How does a server add to a guest's order at a later time or from a different server terminal?
10. For what reason might a restaurant manager decide not to have kitchen printers?
11. What must be done at the computer terminal to settle and close each guest's account?
12. What kinds of computations can the computer system do on the guest checks?

 PROJECTS

1. If you are a waiter or waitress in a restaurant with table service, or if you know a server who will help you, strap on a pedometer and keep track of the miles walked during an eight hour shift. Do this three times and average the results. Calculate how far a server walks in one day on the job without the help of a computer to save steps to the kitchen.
2. Interview a manager whose serving staff uses a restaurant computer. Find out what dining room hardware they use. Write a short paper discussing the step-by-step procedure they follow for using the computer from taking the order to settling a guest's account. Include the backup plan or procedure that the restaurant uses when the computer is inoperative.
3. Compare the system of having a cashier with the system of having servers keep their own receipts. Discuss the advantages and disadvantages of each situation.

8

WINE AND BAR SERVICE

The proper service of alcoholic beverages is very important because many restaurants are merchandising drinks to satisfy the demand of guests and to increase profits. The waiter's or waitress's correct service of alcoholic beverages—wines, beers, and liquors—depends not only on knowing the procedure for serving but also on the knowledge of types of drinks, glassware, beverage temperature, and garnishes. A server should know which beverages complement particular foods on the menu in order to offer suggestions.

▮ SIGNIFICANCE OF SERVING WINE, BEER, AND LIQUOR

Many guests enjoy alcoholic beverages before, with, or after their meals when dining in a restaurant. Wines, beers, and liquors stimulate the appetite of the diner and are palatable companions to all types of foods. They not only make the meal taste better but also add a festive note to the pleasure of dining in a restaurant.

Alcoholic beverages are one of the most profitable moneymakers in the food service business. Because alcoholic beverages add to the customer's check, the server's tip will be higher.

A waiter or waitress should always suggest drinks with every dinner. Suggest a cocktail, appetizer wine, or beer prior to dinner; wine with dinner; and an after-dinner drink following the meal. Specifically asking whether the guest would like drinks and being especially knowledgeable about serving drinks add to your merchandising efforts (see the section on Making Suggestions in Chapter 4).

■■■ THE CONCERN OVER SERVING ALCOHOL IN RESTAURANTS

Restaurant owners are concerned about being held legally responsible for injuries or deaths caused by customers who are too young to drink alcohol and customers who leave their establishments intoxicated. Laws in most states prohibit serving alcohol to underage or intoxicated guests and hold the server, manager, and owner of the restaurant personally liable for the guest's conduct and consequences of excessive drinking.

The server's responsibility is to serve only patrons of legal drinking age. Judging the customer's age is very difficult, and this job often falls directly on the server. A server should verify the age of a young guest by asking for proof of age such as a driver's license with photo or an identification card issued by the state liquor authority. Some restaurants have young guests sign a statement that they are of legal age to consume liquor.

A server must also identify the point at which a guest of legal age should discontinue drinking alcoholic beverages. Ideally, a server should identify the onset of intoxication at an early stage before the problem becomes severe. Usually when the dinner is served, the guest discontinues or slows down the rate of alcohol consumption, and a server will not have a problem. Occasionally, however, a guest does not order dinner and consumes only alcohol, or arrives at the restaurant inebriated. The server's responsibility is to intervene, handle the situation tactfully, and try to maintain the restaurant's good reputation.

The server may be able to identify the degree of intoxication of a guest by monitoring his bar tab and behavior. Table 8–1 from the National Restaurant Association, is a guide to identifying behavior associated with various stages of intoxication. You should try to identify the point between the green and yellow stages. At this point you can stall for time by serving drinks at a slower rate, by quietly suggesting coffee or nonalcoholic wines or drinks, or by tactfully informing the guest you cannot serve him or her another drink. If the customer still insists on another alcoholic drink, turn the problem over to the manager on duty.

Some restaurants promote designated driver programs in which one member of a party of guests who are consuming alcohol is encouraged to refrain from drinking and is designated as the driver for the group. Other restaurants offer free food and taxi rides for drunk customers.

Recognizing the stages of intoxication

Green Level
(no noticeable behavior change)

Customer
- is talkative
- seems relaxed, comfortable, happy

Yellow Level
(relaxed inhibitions and impaired judgment)

Customer
- becomes louder or more talkative
- becomes more quiet
- behaves in an overly friendly way
- curses at the server's slow service
- complains that drinks are getting weaker
- insists on singing with the band

Red Level
(loss of motor coordination)

Customer
- spills a drink
- sways when walking
- has slurred speech
- asks for a double
- is unable to pick up change
- annoys or argues with other customers
- becomes tearful or drowsy
- has difficulty focusing
- falls or stumbles

Table 8–1   Recognizing the stages of intoxication.

A reputation for careful practices regarding alcohol service, in addition to conscientious waiters or waitresses, is a restaurant's best defense in a third-party liability case.

◼️ WINE SERVICE

WINE MERCHANDISING

Wine is an alcoholic beverage made by fermenting the juice of grapes. It is an important part of the American dining tradition. Traditional wine service is given with much showmanship, and therefore, the server needs to be fully informed in all aspects of wine service. Many restaurants have wine lists on the table or have the server present the wine list to the guest. Often displays of wine bottles in the restaurant and the presence of wine glasses on the table subtly suggest wine as part of the meal. As a waiter or waitress, you should be ready to present and serve wine in the time-honored tradition if the customer would like it.

CHARACTERISTICS OF WINE

Wines are identified by color, body, bouquet, taste, name, and vintage. As a waiter or waitress, you should be knowledgeable about wines and be able to distinguish one wine from another for your guests.

Wines are either white or red in accordance with age, grape variety, and the length of time the grape skins are left in the grape juice while it is fermenting to form wine. White wines are made by fermenting the grape juice without skins. Pink wines (rosé and blush) are made by separating the skins soon after fermentation has begun. The skins remain in the tank to make reds. White wines range from almost crystal clear to gold to amber in color, and red wines range from pink to red to crimson. Rosé wines are pink table wines and share characteristics of both red and white table wines, as do the blush wines. Rosé wines are generally blended wines whereas blush wines are sweeter and are made from one grape variety.

Body describes the thickness or thinness of the wine. The body of wine is determined by how it flows around the inside of a glass as it is swirled. A light wine flows quickly, and full-bodied wine flows slowly.

The *bouquet* or aroma or fragrance a wine emits as it is swirled is one of the most sensational qualities of a wine. For example, the bouquet may be fruity or flowery. Red wines need to rest or breathe for several minutes after they are opened to develop their bouquet.

The flavor of each wine ranges from very dry (not sweet) to very sweet. Complete fermentation produces a dry wine. A sweet wine is produced by interrupting the fermentation process. The dryness or sweetness characteristic usually determines when the wine is served during the meal (see the section on Wines and Foods That Complement Each Other later in this chapter).

Wines may be named and identified on their labels by their varietal, generic, or proprietary names. Wines are often numbered on wine lists because names of wines are difficult to pronounce. A description of names on labels follows:

- A wine with a varietal name has the name of the primary grape used in making the wine. California law states that at least 51 percent of the juice in a wine must come from the named variety of grape. Some wines contain up to 100 percent of the named grape. Examples of wines with varietal names are Pinot Noir and Chardonnay.

- Some wines are known by their generic names. These wines are named after the geographic region where the grapes are grown. Burgundy and

Champagne are wines with generic names. American-made wines similar to the originals sometimes bear the generic name of the wine they resemble. For example, New York Champagne bears resemblance to French Champagne, and California Burgundy is similar to Burgundy from France.

- Wines may have proprietary names that are brand names adopted by the bottler for sales purposes. These names do not conform to other classifications.

Wines are produced in many countries. France, Germany, and Italy are important wine producers, as are Switzerland, Spain, Portugal, Austria, Hungary, Greece, Yugoslavia, and others.

The United States is a major wine producer. Most United States wines come from California, New York, Ohio, Maryland, and Michigan. American and European wines do not taste the same even when they are made from the same grapes. The difference in taste is caused by different climates, soils, and growing conditions.

Vintage refers to the year that the grapes were harvested, and many wines carry the year of the harvest on their labels. In European countries, the vintage year statement is used to identify the occurrence of years when the weather in the vineyard districts had been sunny enough to fully ripen the grapes. In California, the long, rainless summers permit the grapes to mature every year, but the state's wines still reflect subtle changes in the weather from year to year. In order to state a vintage year on the label, the United States requires that 95 percent of the grapes in a wine be grown and fermented during that year. Wineries in other countries do not enforce this law allowing for some very fine wines to be undated.

TYPES OF WINE

Wines are grouped into four basic types: table, sparkling, fortified, and aromatized.

1. **Table wines**. All unfortified white and red wines that normally accompany a meal are referred to as *table wines*. The alcohol content of table wines is 9.5 to 14 percent. They are created entirely by the natural fermentation of sugars in grape juice. Some examples of table wines are Burgundy and Bordeaux.

2. **Sparkling wines**. Sparkling wines, often used for special occasions, contain 8 to 14 percent alcohol. Carbon dioxide is added to make these wines effervescent. Champagne is a well-known sparkling wine.

3. **Fortified wines**. Fortified wines are wines that are combined with brandy to increase the alcohol content to within 17 to 22 percent. Fortified wines can vary from dry to sweet. For example, a dry sherry can be used as an aperitif wine, and a sweet sherry or port can be served as a dessert wine.

4. **Aromatized wines**. A few wines are lightly fortified and flavored with herbs, spices, and peels. Aromatized wines, such as vermouth, are often served in combination with other alcoholic beverages as cocktails. Aromatized wines contain between 15 and 20 percent alcohol.

TEMPERATURE OF WINE

The flavor of red wine is at its best at room temperature (60 to 65°F), and white, rosé, and blush wines are best served chilled (45 to 50°F). Sparkling wines should also be served chilled (35 to 40°F). Serving the wine at the correct temperature is the waiter's or waitress's responsibility, unless otherwise requested by the guests.

Prior to service, all wines should be stored in a cool, dark location (Figure 8–1). An ideal wine storage temperature for a long period of time is approximately 55°F. Wines with corks should be stored horizontally so the corks do not dry out and crumble into the bottle or allow air to enter and spoil the wine.

Before serving white, rosé, blush, and sparkling wines, chill them one or two hours in the refrigerator. To maintain a constant supply of chilled wines, some restaurants keep a number of bottles cold in the refrigerator at the bar. The server then gets the chilled bottle ordered by guests from the bartender and replaces it with a bottle of the same wine from storage to be chilled for another time. Wines may be chilled in a refrigerator for up to two weeks; a

Figure 8–1 Bottles should be stored horizontally in a cool, dark location to prevent the corks from drying out and to preserve the quality of the wine.

longer period of chilling destroys the flavor. Wines that have been in the refrigerator the longest should be used first. Never freeze or warm up a wine.

In some restaurants, a wine cooler or ice bucket may be used to maintain the proper temperature of wine at the table. Partly fill the bucket with ice and water so that the bottle slips in and out easily. Because this cooler is mainly for showmanship and maintenance of temperature, prechilling wine in a refrigerator is still advisable.

Under normal conditions, red wines do not need chilling prior to service. To slightly lower the temperature, you may wish to chill the wine for five minutes in the refrigerator.

WINES AND FOODS THAT COMPLEMENT EACH OTHER

No hard and fast rules define which wine complements a certain food, although time, tradition, and common sense have given us certain wine and food associations. Therefore, any wine may be served with any food and be correct.

The waiter and waitress should serve the wine ordered by the guests and never criticize a guest's selection. When a guest asks your opinion, however, suggest a wine that is traditionally acceptable with the food ordered. Table 8–2 illustrates some well-accepted combinations of wines and foods that complement each other. Notice that dry, light wines are usually served at the beginning of the meal. As the meal progresses, medium-dry wines are served with the entrée. Delicate wines go well with delicate dishes and full-bodied wines go well with robust foods (Figure 8–2). Only with dessert should sweet wines be served. When only one wine is desired with the meal and when guests order a variety of entrées at the same table, suggest a rosé wine.

THE AMOUNT OF WINE TO ORDER

Most bottles of wine are fifths (25.6 ounces). The number of servings per fifth depends on the size of the wine glass used. Generally, a fifth is enough for six four-ounce servings. Wines in restaurants are also sold in half-bottles (splits) and by the glass. A good rule of thumb for ordering wine is a half bottle for two persons, a full bottle for three to six persons, and two bottles for seven to twelve persons. Knowing the approximate number of servings enables you to suggest the appropriate amount for your party of guests to order.

WINE GLASSES

A wine glass is traditionally a stemmed, tulip-shaped glass. The stemmed feature allows the guest to hold a glass by the stem so the wine is not warmed by the heat of his or her hands. The glass should be large enough to allow the guest to swirl the wine and smell the bouquet (aroma), which is part of the pleasure of wine drinking. The bowl of the glass should be clear and free of decoration so that the color and clarity of the wine is visible.

.Usually the restaurant has several kinds of wine glasses suitable for serving different types of wine. With each new type of wine ordered, a clean, appro-

Type of Wine	Particular Wine	Characteristics	Foods they Compliment
White Wines	Muscadet Chablis Graves Sauvignon Blanc	Light to medium-bodied, dry	Mild cheeses, appetizers, seafood, tuna, light pasta
	Riesling Liebfraumilch	Light to medium-bodied, lightly sweet	Poultry, Asian foods, pork, veal, ham
	Pinot Blanc Chardonnay	Medium to full-bodied, dry	Seafood with sauces, tuna, poultry, pork, veal, ham
	Sauternes	Medium to full-bodied, sweet	Strong cheeses, fruits, desserts
Red Wines	Valpolicella Gamay Beaujolais Chianti Côtes du Rhône	Light to medium bodied, dry	Nuts, cheeses, appetizers, pizza, tomato pasta, salmon, tuna, poultry, game, pork, veal, ham, beef, simply prepared meats
	Pinot Noir Merlot Zinfandel Cabernet Sauvignon Barolo Barbaresco	Medium to full-bodied, dry	Strong cheeses, hearty pasta, beef and lamb cuts, barbeque
Rosé and Blush Wines	Grenache Rosé White Zinfandel	Light to medium-bodied	Luncheon foods, Asian foods, seafood, salmon, tuna, poultry, light pasta, pork, veal, ham, fruits, dessert
Sparkling Wines	Champagne Sparkling Burgundy		All foods, especially lighter foods and meats, desserts

Table 8–2   Wines and foods that complement each other.

priate glass should be provided. Appetizer and dessert wines are often served in a three- to five-ounce stemmed glass. Dinner wines are served in a larger glass, ranging from 6 to 12 ounces. Sometimes the glass for red wine is larger than the glass for white wine. In this case, the glass for the red wine is a 9- to 12-ounce glass, and the glass for white wine is the smaller 7- to 9-ounce glass. White wine is served in smaller portions to allow it to be consumed while retaining its chilled temperature, while the remainder of the bottle stays chilled in the ice bucket. Although champagne traditionally was served in a saucer-shaped, stemmed glass, today a narrow, tulip-shaped glass is preferred because it allows the wine to generate bubbles longer. A 7- to 8-ounce, tulip-shaped glass is an all-purpose wine glass suitable for all types of wine.

Figure 8–2   Pinot Noir, a red dinner wine, complements a salmon entrée.

Wine glasses may vary in shape and design, depending on the decor of the restaurant and the preferences of management. Some traditional wine glasses used in restaurants are shown in Figure 8–3.

WINE LISTS, WINE CHARTS, AND JUG WINES

A wine list is a wine menu. A restaurateur works closely with a local wine distributor to place on the list dependable domestic and foreign wines that complement the food menu. A balanced wine list is made up of red, white, sweet, sparkling, rosé, and sometimes blush wines. A good wine list is brief and describes the wines and foods they complement. It is generally kept simple because the average guest recognizes only a few of the more popular wines. For some customers, a wine list may include several expensive wines, but generally the wines on the wine list are priced at no more than the average price of a dinner.

Figure 8–3   Frequently used wine glasses are the all-purpose wine, champagne saucer, champagne tulip, and sherry glasses.

A good waiter or waitress reads the complete wine list and learns how to pronounce the wines in order to communicate them to the customers. Some restaurants have wine charts carried by servers that describe available wines and pairs them with menu items. Most charts include the wine list number, name, phonetic pronunciation, year, bottle size, price, type, origin, serving temperature, characteristics, and foods the wines complement. A good wine chart shows whether the wine is light or full-bodied, sweet or dry. Your restaurant should have plenty of copies of the wine list on hand. These lists should be located in a convenient place and kept in good condition; messy, untidy copies with written-in changes should not be used.

In addition to bottle wines on a wine list, restaurateurs are turning more frequently toward California and Italian red, white, rosé, or blush jug wines for bar and house wines. These wines are easy to sell by the carafe, half-carafe, or glass. Many customers, especially those unfamiliar with wines, still prefer to be asked, "Will you have a carafe of our house wine?" rather than be offered a wine list with unfamiliar names.

TAKING THE WINE ORDER

After becoming familiar with the wine list, you will feel comfortable taking the wine order. Bring out the wine lists with the menus and distribute them around the table. When only one wine list is available per table ask, "Who will be interested in ordering the wine tonight?" Then open the wine list and hand it to the host or hostess of the table.

Figure 8–4   The bottle of wine should be carefully carried to the table and presented to the host or hostess so the label can be read.

Take the wine order after you take the food order. You might sense a feeling of unfamiliarity with the wine list, and in this case you might suggest, "Our California Riesling is excellent with the broiled trout you ordered," or "We have a very good house rosé served in a carafe."

When the wine order has been taken, serve the wine according to the time given to you by the host or hostess. If he or she has given no instructions regarding when the wine is to be served, then open and serve a white, rosé, or blush wine with the first course. Open red wines immediately also, but present them to the host or hostess and then set them on the table. The bouquet is allowed to develop and then the red wine can be served with the entrée. Then thank the guests, collect the wine lists with the menus, and continue with the service.

PROCEDURE FOR OPENING AND SERVING WINE

Serve wine in the proper manner, with a great deal of showmanship, so that the guests get the greatest enjoyment from it as follows.

Opening Red Wines. Obtain the bottle of wine of the right temperature and carefully carry it to the table. From the right side, present the bottle to the host or hostess by showing the label (Figure 8–4). State the name of the wine, such as "The Burgundy you ordered, sir (or ma'am)." Wait for approval. Then place the bottle of red wine on the table to be opened.

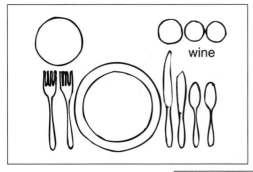

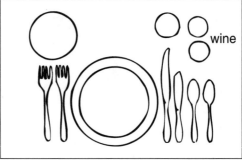

Figure 8–5 Either way of placing wine glasses shown here is proper when more than one kind of wine is to be served with the meal.

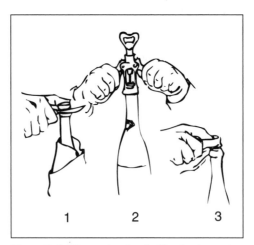

Figure 8–6 Open a bottle of table wine by cutting away the foil and wiping away the mold, removing the cork with a corkscrew, and wiping the lip of the bottle again before pouring from it.

The correct wine glasses are brought next so that guests may anticipate the wine service. Set each wine glass on the table to the right of and slightly below the water glass. When serving several wines, either place the glasses in a line to the right of the water glass or place one wine glass below the other (Figure 8–5).

Handle the bottle carefully so any sediment in it is not stirred up. Cut around the lower lip of the bottle and remove the foil. Wipe away any mold that has formed near the cork. Press on the cork slightly to break the seal between the cork and the bottle. Using one of the many varieties of corkscrews (especially popular is a lever-type corkscrew called the *waiter's corkscrew*), insert the spiral screw into the cork and twist it until only one or two turns of the screw are visible. Using the lever or handles, remove the cork from the bottle (Figure 8–6). Smell the cork to detect any musty, vinegary, or sulfuric odor that indicates the wine is not good. If the cork has an off-smell, replace the bottle with another at once. If the wine is good, remove the cork from the corkscrew and place it on the table to the right of the host's or hostess's glass and proceed.

Wipe the lip of the bottle. Pour a sample of the wine into the host's or hostess's glass. Once it has been tasted and approved, place the open bottle in the center of the table to develop the bouquet. Always face the label out when opening or pouring so that guests can see it.

Pour the wine for the guests when the entrée is served. Leaving each glass on the table, fill the glasses one-half to two-thirds full, twisting the bottle a quarter turn as you finish pouring to prevent dripping. Pour the wine for the woman at the host's or hostess's right and continue counterclockwise, serving all the women in the party. Then serve the men, serving the host or hostess last. Never completely empty a bottle because you may pour out the sediment at the bottom. If the proper amount of wine has been ordered, there will be enough wine for each guest. Place the remaining wine on the table to the right of the host or hostess. Be available to refill glasses as needed. You may wish to suggest another bottle.

Opening White, Blush, and Rosé Wines   When white, blush, or rosé wines are ordered, bring the chilled bottle to the table in a bucket of crushed ice and water and place it on a stand to the right of the host or hostess. Present the bottle by showing him or her the label and wait for approval. Then place the chilled wine back in the ice bucket.

Bring the wine glasses next. Set each wine glass on the table to the right of and slightly below the water glass. When serving several wines, either place the glasses in a line to the right of the water glass or place one wine glass below the other, as shown in Figure 8–5.

Open the wine in the ice bucket to keep it chilled. Cut around the lower lip of the bottle and remove the foil covering the top of the cork. Wipe away any mold that has formed near the cork. Press on the cork slightly to break the seal between the cork and the bottle. Using a corkscrew, insert the spiral screw into the cork and twist it until only one or two turns of the screw are visible. Using the lever or handles of the corkscrew, remove the cork from the bottle. Smell the cork to be sure the wine is good. Replace a wine with a musty, vinegary, or sulfuric smell with another bottle. If the wine is good, remove the cork from the corkscrew and place it on the table to the right of the host's or hostess's glass.

Wipe the lip of the bottle with a clean napkin. Pour a sample of the wine for the host or hostess and wait for approval.

Pour white, blush, or rosé wines as soon as they are opened and approved by the host or hostess. Wrap the chilled bottle in a clean napkin to maintain its temperature. Allow the label to show. Pour glasses one-half to two-thirds full and twist the bottle as you finish pouring to prevent dripping.

Pour the wine for the woman at the host's or hostess's right and continue counterclockwise to serve all the women in the party. Then serve the men, serving the host or hostess last.

Place the bottle with the remainder of the wine back into the ice bucket so that it will remain chilled. When removing the bottle from the ice and water to refill glasses, wipe the water from the outside so you do not drip water on a guest or the table.

Opening Sparkling Wines As with white, blush, or rosé wines, keep the chilled bottle of sparkling wine in an ice bucket at the host's or hostess's right. Bring wine glasses next, as described previously. To open the wine, wrap the bottle in a clean cloth napkin to maintain its chilled temperature and protect your hands from possible glass breakage. Cut the foil below the wire and remove it. Untwist the wire with your right hand while holding your left thumb on top of the cork. Remove the wire. Continuing to hold in the cork with your left thumb, tilt the bottle at a 45 degree angle and point it away from the guests. Firmly hold the cork with your left hand, and twist the bottle with your right hand. Let pressure escape slowly. Allow the pressure in the bottle to force the cork out gently without a pop or fizz (Figure 8–7). Remove the napkin from the bottle and serve the host or hostess a taste. When given approval, serve the rest of the guests as you did with table wines.

■■■ BEER SERVICE

TYPES OF BEER

Beer is a term referring to a brewed alcoholic beverage made from fermented barley malt, hops, yeast, and water with an alcoholic strength of two to six percent. In the United States, most of the beer consumed is a *lager beer*, a generic term for a pale, aged, effervescent brew introduced from Germany during the middle of the last century. In addition to malt, other grains such

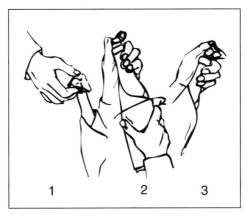

Figure 8–7 Open a bottle of sparkling wine by first removing the foil and wire. Then grasp the cork and tilt the bottle away from the guest. While holding the cork firmly, twist the bottle to allow the internal pressure to push the cork out.

as corn and rice are frequently used to give lager its light body. All lager beers are aged by storing them for several months before putting them into bottles, cans, or kegs.

Ale is another generic form of beer that differs from lager beer in that it has a different proportion of beer ingredients and is fermented at a higher temperature. These differences in brewing make ale a heavier beer with a more pronounced flavor of hops and a higher alcohol content.

Types of beer have certain characteristics. For instance, *pilsner* is a lager beer with a pale, golden color, a strong hops flavor, and an alcohol content of 4.5 to 5.0 percent. *Munchener* is a beer made in Munich, Germany. It is deep brown in color and slightly sweet and has a strong malt flavor. *Weisse,* a white beer, is a German beer made from wheat. It is light and very refreshing. *Malt liquors* are lager beers with an alcohol content range of four to six percent. *Light beer* is a lager specially brewed to reduce the number of carbohydrates and calories in it. Once a year, American and European brewers make a Bock beer and offer it in the spring. *Bock* is a dark beer with more body than usual and the added pleasant bitterness that comes from hops.

TYPES OF BEER GLASSES

Beer may be served in a mug, pilsner, goblet, schooner, tumbler, shell, stein, or hourglass tumbler. Pictured in Figure 8–8 are a footed pilsner—a tall, narrow, seven-ounce glass with a short stem—and a stein—a heavy glass with a handle. Beer glasses must he spotlessly clean, with no greasy film, or the beer in them will go flat.

Figure 8–8   A footed pilsner and a stein are two of the many glasses used to serve beer.

PROCEDURE FOR SERVING BEER

Beer goes well with almost any food served in a restaurant except sweets. Beer may be served before the meal with the appetizer, during the meal, and as a beverage any time. The taste of the beer is at its best at about 40°F.

The glass is placed on the table to the right and below the water glass, and the beer is poured for the guest. Do not tip the glass or pick it up from the table, but pour from the bottle directly into the center of the glass to release the carbon dioxide and form a head of foam. Most of the rules for serving beverages (see Chapter 5, Serving the Meal) apply to serving beer.

■ LIQUOR SERVICE

TYPES OF LIQUOR

Cocktails, mixed drinks, and straight drinks are made from brandy, whiskey, vodka, gin, rum, cordials, and other liquors and spirits. As a server, you should be familiar with the following spirits, which are the most frequently ordered.

1. *Brandy* is liquor made by the distillation of wine or a fermented fruit mash. The word *brandy* by itself refers to the liquor that is made from grape wine. Kirsch (cherry brandy), applejack (apple brandy), and apri-

cot brandy are examples of fruit brandy. A well-known brandy is cognac, which is distilled in the region near the city of Cognac, France.

2. *Whiskey* is a liquor distilled from fermented grain mash and aged in wooden barrels. The grain, yeast, water, and blending of whiskey have a lot to do with the flavor and lightness of the spirit.

   Most restaurant bars stock straight, blended, and bonded whiskeys that vary in age, alcoholic content, and flavor characteristics. Bourbon is a well-known straight whiskey. American, Canadian, Scotch, and Irish whiskey are the main whiskeys sold in the United States.

3. *Vodka* is usually distilled from grain mash but is not aged, as are many other spirits. It is colorless and has no aroma or flavor. Because of its neutral character it is usually served blended with fruit juices, spirits, or wines.

4. *Gin* is a redistilled liquor employing the juniper berry as the principal flavoring agent. Other flavoring agents are roots, herbs, peels, and other berries. Gin is a dry spirit used in many popular drinks.

5. *Rum* is a by-product of sugar manufacturing; thus, most rums are distilled in the tropics. Rums range from the very dark Jamaican rums to the light, delicately-flavored rums from Cuba and Puerto Rico. Rums are used for cooking and in many drinks.

6. Other liquors include *aquavit*, a Scandinavian distilled beverage made exactly the same way as gin but with a caraway flavor, and *tequila*, a Mexican spirit distilled from pulque, the juice of the agave.

7. *Cordials* are sweet, colorful drinks which must contain at least two percent sugar. In Europe, cordials are called *liqueurs*. They are made by various processes that allow brandy to absorb the coloring, flavor and aroma of fruits, leaves, and peels. Well-known cordials include crème de cacao, Benedictine, Chartreuse, Drambuie, crème de menthe, and Triple Sec.

TEMPERATURE OF DRINKS

Almost all cocktails, mixed drinks, and straight drinks must he served very cold. In some restaurants, the glasses are prechilled to maintain the cold temperature.

LIQUOR GLASSWARE

Glasses vary in size and style depending on the preference of management. However, the well-known types of glasses are important for the waiter or waitress to recognize.

- *Whiskey jigger or shot glass*   A very small glass with a capacity of 1/2 ounces
- *Highball glass*   A medium-tall, straight-sided glass holding between five and eight ounces

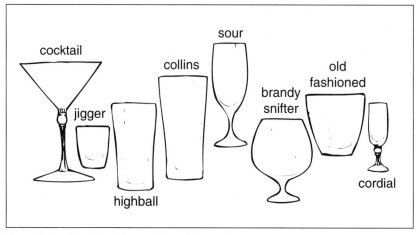

Figure 8–9   Examples of frequently used liquor glasses.

- *Collins glass*   A tall, straight-sided, frosted glass holding about 10 to 12 ounces
- *Old-fashioned glass*   A low, squat glass holding about six ounces
- *Cocktail glass*   A four-ounce, funnel-shaped, stemmed glass
- *Sour glass*   A four-ounce, slender tulip-shaped glass with a short stem
- *Brandy snifter*   An eight-ounce, balloon-shaped glass with a short stem
- *Cordial glass*   A slender stemmed, tulip-shaped glass holding about one ounce

Many cocktails are served *up*, or without ice, in a stemmed glass to prevent the guest's hands from warming the beverage. However, if the guest orders a cocktail *on-the-rocks*, serve the cocktail over cubes of ice in an old-fashioned glass. Some of the liquor glasses used in restaurants are shown in Figure 8–9.

POPULAR COCKTAILS AND MIXED DRINKS

To serve cocktails or mixed drinks properly, the waiter or waitress must have a knowledge of popular drinks (Figure 8–10). Table 8–3 shows the glass, ice, ingredients, and garnish for the drinks frequently ordered in restaurants.

PROCEDURE FOR SERVING DRINKS

After the guests are seated and receive their menus, take the cocktail order. Because of the many drink variations, the waiter or waitress must take the order correctly. Many guests request a particular brand of liquor in their

Figure 8–10 A good waiter or waitress should have a knowledge of popular drinks such as the ones shown here on a tray.

drinks, a variation of mixers (club soda, water, ginger ale, and so on), a different liquor than traditionally used, or a special garnish. For example, a guest may order a vodka gimlet instead of a gin gimlet or a twist instead of an olive in a dry martini.

After you have properly taken the bar order, submit it to the bartender at the service bar, which is an area of the bar for server and bartender use only. You may be required to assist the bartender in preparing the drinks by setting the appropriate glasses on the cocktail tray, icing the glasses when required, adding the mixers, or garnishing the cocktails. Place the drinks on the tray in the order that you took the orders to help you serve the correct drink to each customer. In some restaurants, the policy is to set up ingredients for highballs, on-the-rocks drinks, and straight drinks at the service bar and to combine the ingredients later at the table in front of the guests.

When drink ingredients are combined in front of the guests at the table, pour the measured liquor into the proper glass, then add the proper amount of mixer designated by the guest. When on-the-rocks drinks are prepared in front of the guests, pour the liquor over the ice in the glass.

When drinks are ready to serve, apply the ordinary rules of serving beverages. Serve from the right with the right hand, and serve women first. Place the drink to the right and slightly below the water glass. Remove drink glasses when empty. Ask the guests if they would like another cocktail before ordering the meal.

After the guests complete the entrée or dessert and the soiled dishes are cleared, suggest an after-dinner drink such as brandy or a cordial. Serve them in the same manner as you serve other cocktails and mixed drinks.

Drink	Glass	Ice	Ingredients	Garnish
Manhattan	cocktail	stir with ice, then strain into glass	whiskey; sweet vermouth	maraschino cherry
Dry Manhattan	cocktail	stir with ice, then strain into glass	whiskey; dry vermouth	olive
Dry Martini	cocktail	stir with ice, then strain into glass	gin; dry vermouth	olive
Bloody Mary	high-ball	cubes in glass	vodka; tomato juice; hot pepper sauce; Worcester-shire sauce	–
Daiquiri	cocktail	blend with ice	rum; sugar; lime juice	lime or filbert
Gimlet	cocktail	stir with ice, then strain into glass	gin; lime juice	lime or filbert
Old Fashioned	old fash-ioned	cubes in glass	whiskey; sugar; bitters	½ orange slice; maraschino cherry
Screwdriver	high-ball	cubes in glass	vodka; orange juice	–
Tom Collins	collins	blend with ice	gin; lemon juice; pow-dered sugar	½ orange slice; maraschino cherry
Whiskey Sour	sour	blend with ice	whiskey; lemon juice; sugar	½ orange slice; maraschino cherry

Table 8–3 Recognizing popular drinks.

MOCKTAILS

As guests become increasingly concerned about nutrition, weight control, and driving while intoxicated, they are shifting their tastes to lighter drinks such as low- or no-alcohol beers and wines and other beverages without alcohol. One of the biggest innovations in bar drinks has been nonalcoholic beverages called *mocktails*. These drinks are alcohol-free but contain other bar ingredients such as fruit juice and mixers. They may be concocted and garnished to resemble alcoholic drinks such as coolers, fruit fizzes, frappés and ice cream-based smoothies. A popular mocktail expression is a *virgin drink* which is an alcohol-free drink, such as a Virgin Mary—a Bloody Mary without vodka.

 QUESTIONS

1. What are the advantages of serving alcoholic beverages in a restaurant?
2. What are the restaurant personnel's responsibilities in regard to serving minors or intoxicated guests?
3. How do blush wines differ from rosé?
4. What is the *bouquet* of a wine? How does the server get the red wine bouquet to develop?
5. When are dry wines and sweet wines usually served during the meal?
6. What does the vintage tell you about wines?
7. Why should corked wines be stored horizontally?
8. What is the maximum time that wine should be refrigerated?
9. Why is an ice bucket or wine cooler used in the service of wine?
10. What wines would you suggest with the following foods: lasagne, prime rib, shrimp cocktail, chicken, cheesecake, lobster, cheese soufflé, sirloin steak, chef's salad?
11. What amount of wine (fifth, split, glass) would you suggest for two people? Six people? Twelve people?
12. Why are wine glasses stemmed?
13. Why should a bottle of wine be handled with care before opening it?
14. What purpose does a wine chart serve?
15. What is the procedure for pouring beer for the guest?
16. What are the distinguishing features of brandy, whiskey, vodka, gin, rum, and cordials?
17. Why is it important to know the glassware used for alcoholic beverages?
18. What are some of the ingredients found in a mocktail?

PROJECTS

1. From your restaurant's wine list or any wine list, identify the types of wine listed, such as table, sparkling, fortified, and aromatized. Determine the temperature at which you would serve each wine. Ask a bartender to answer any questions you might have about the wine list.

2. Attend a short, commentated tasting of wines on a good wine list. Note the qualities of each wine. You can read many books on wine, but nothing replaces firsthand tasting of the wine in question. You as the server are most likely to encourage customers to try the wines *you* have tasted and liked.

3. Obtain examples of glassware used for drinks, and list the drinks that are served in each glass.

4. Memorize the table of popular drinks in this manual and learn those drinks popular in your area. Identify the setup, including the glassware, ice, and garnish, as a fellow trainee names each drink.

5. Role-play serving alcoholic beverages. Ask some of the trainees to be guests. Practice suggesting drinks, taking the order, opening and serving table wines and sparkling wines, and serving beer, cocktails and mixed drinks (including combining drinks at the table).

CASE PROBLEMS

▬▬▬ CASE 1   INITIATING THE SERVICE

A female executive is seated with her male client in your station at 1:00 P.M. She tells you they are celebrating the culmination of a large business deal and they are ready to relax after a month of hard work. They are discussing the menu and the executive is considering ordering a shrimp cocktail (an appetizer) as her lunch. Her guest is considering a pasta entrée and side salad selection. A topic of conversation is calories and how they both like to maintain healthy eating habits. They seem to have plenty of time to enjoy their lunch.

- What signs do you look for to identify the host or hostess? In this case, who would you approach?
- What words would you use to initiate the service?
- How would you use suggestive selling?
- How would you time this meal?
- To whom would you present the check?

■■■■ CASE 2   A SENSITIVE SITUATION

A customer is smoking in a nonsmoking area, and others in the area are offended by the smoke and ask you to intercede. You as a server must deal with the problem since there is a state law requiring restaurants to have an area that is smoke free. The customer, who is smoking, is intoxicated. When you confront the lady who is smoking, she states that you are discriminating against her because of her ethnic background.

- What steps could you take as the server to calm this person down?
- If she continues to make a scene, what additional steps could you as a server do?
- If your supervisor suddenly became available, what steps could be taken to reduce the tense situation and still meet the requirements of the law?

■■■■ CASE 3   HANDLING HARASSMENT

You are approached by your supervisor who makes remarks with sexual overtones while you are working as a server. You are made to feel uncomfortable by these remarks. The state where you are working has strong sexual harassment laws and you are aware of them. You feel you want to curtail this situation before it leads to something you do not want to happen.

- What are your rights?
- What steps can you take to make sure your supervisor understands your feelings and that you can continue your job in that establishment?
- Who can you report this situation to if it goes beyond your control?

▉▉▉▉ CASE 4   BAD SUGGESTION

A server makes a recommendation about a wine and the guest decides to try it. The wine is brought to the table, opened, and, according to custom, a sample is poured for the host. He tastes it but does not like it, saying it is "acidic" instead of "soft" as you described.

- Who should take responsibility for the rejected bottle of wine?
- Why did this happen?
- What are the exact words you would use to convey to the guest that you understand his objection to the wine?
- Would you take back the wine?

WAITER AND WAITRESS QUIZ

PART A COMPLETION

Fill in the blank(s) with the correct word or words to complete the sentence.

1. A garment that identifies the occupation of the wearer is a(n) __________.
2. The most important goals of any restaurant are to satisfy the customer and make a(n) __________.
3. The arrangement of china, silverware, napkin, and glassware at each place setting is called a(n) __________.
4. The silverware in the American breakfast and lunch cover is set so the __________ is to the left of the napkin and the __________ and __________ are to the right of the napkin.
5. In American service, the water glass is placed above the tip of the __________.
6. A section of the dining room that has seating for a dozen or more guests at tables, booths, or counter seats and is assigned to one waiter or waitress is a(n) __________.
7. A second tablecloth or padding beneath the top tablecloth is called a(n) __________.
8. A leftover, seasonal dish, or chefs specialty is called a(n) __________.
9. Condiments, decorative garnishes, and foods that complement the entrée are called __________.
10. Stand to the __________ of the guest when taking orders.
11. Making suggestions benefits the restaurant by increasing the size of the check and benefits the server by increasing the size of the __________.
12. If guests at a table order beef burgundy, filet mignon, lobster newburg, and ribs of beef, you would submit the __________ order to the kitchen first, followed by the other three orders, so all four orders are done at the same time.
13. Food is served from the __________ of the guest with the __________ hand, and beverages are served from the __________ of the guest with the __________ hand.

14. A small plate placed beneath fruit, juice, seafood cocktails, and some beverages is called a(n) _____.

15. Clear dishes from the _____ of the guests with the _____ hand.

16. Stack dishes on trays so that they are _____.

17. After eating, drinking, smoking, or using the restroom, and to prevent food contamination, a server should _____.

18. Your main responsibility in an emergency is to encourage everyone to _____.

19. The physical components of a computer system that accept and process the information fed into them at a restaurant are called _____.

20. Computer point-of-sale machines with keyboards are referred to as _____.

21. Machines that imprint information on food and beverage orders, guest checks, receipts, and management reports are known as _____.

22. Wines that are not sweet are _____ wines.

23. The year of the grape harvest is called the _____.

24. If the guest orders the cocktail _____, serve the cocktail over cubes of ice in an old-fashioned glass, and if the guest orders the cocktail _____, serve it without ice in a cocktail glass.

25. Beer goes well with almost any food except _____.

■■■ PART B   MULTIPLE CHOICE

Circle the letter of the answer that best completes the statement.

1. The willingness to work with coworkers in a common effort toward completing the work assigned is the qualification of being (**a**) reliable, (**b**) personable, (**c**) cooperative, (**d**) healthy.

2. A type of jewelry that may be worn with your uniform is a (**a**) bracelet, (**b**) watch, (**c**) brooch, (**d**) necklace.

3. In a traditional organizational structure, a waiter or waitress reports directly to the (**a**) owner (**b**) steward, (**c**) maitre d'hôtel, (**d**) head-waiter or head waitress.

4. French service is characterized by (**a**) food being plated in the kitchen, (**b**) food being dished up on plates by the host, (**c**) food being cooked in front of the guest and served by two waiters, (**d**) food being served from large platters by one waiter.

5. The type of service in which the menu, number of guests, and time of service are predetermined in advance is a (an) (**a**) banquet, (**b**) buffet, (**c**) family-style dinner (**d**) English-style dinner.

6. Smorgasbord service is similar to (**a**) banquet service, (**b**) buffet service, (**c**) French service, (**d**) English service.

7. A sidestand is a (**a**) tray stand, (**b**) coat rack, (**c**) storage and service unit, (**d**) waiter and waitress lounge.

8. When food on a menu is a la carte, it is (**a**) served from a cart, (**b**) served with a beverage, (**c**) priced to include an entire meal, (**d**) listed as a single item and priced separately from other food items.

9. Closing the dining room involves such duties as (**a**) asking the remaining guests to leave, (**b**) setting up the tables for the next morning's business, (**c**) discarding voided checks, (**d**) turning off all heating equipment such as roll warmers and coffee urns.

10. A greeter should (**a**) avoid seating two groups in the same station at the same time, (**b**) seat large families at deuces, (**c**) seat smokers wherever they would like to be seated, (**d**) leave extra table settings in case others join the group at the table.

11. To place the order in the kitchen the server should (**a**) orally communicate it to the chef, (**b**) hand the guest check or hand written order to the chef, (**c**) key it into a computer terminal, (**d**) all of the above.

12. The sequence of serving the courses during a meal is as follows: (**a**) appetizer, dessert, entrée, salad; (**b**) salad, appetizer entrée, dessert; (**c**) entrée, appetizer, salad, dessert; (**d**) appetizer, salad, entrée, dessert.

13. To serve booths: (**a**) serve the guest farthest from you first with the hand farthest from the guest, (**b**) serve the guest farthest from you first with the hand closest to the guest, (**c**) serve the guest closest to you first with the hand farthest from the guest, (**d**) serve the guest closest to you first with the hand closest to the guest.

14. When serving more than one table, choose the order of serving the following foods from your tray so that proper food temperatures will he maintained: (**a**) ice cream, crackers, hot rolls, (**b**) crackers, ice cream, hot rolls, (**c**) hot rolls, crackers, ice cream, (**d**) ice cream, hot rolls, crackers.

15. Two ways a guest check may he presented to the customer are: (**a**) face down on the table and face down on a tip tray, (**b**) face up on the table and face up on a tip tray, (**c**) face up on the table and face down on a tip tray, (**d**) face down on the table and face up on a tip tray.

16. An example of an unsafe practice is to (**a**) pass coworkers on the right in the aisles between tables, (**b**) keep emergency exits unlocked, (**c**) pour coffee refills while the guest is holding the cup, (**d**) bend your knees when you lift a heavy tray.

17. An example of an unsanitary practice is to (**a**) steady the pitcher on the rim of the glass when pouring water refills, (**b**) replace a utensil that has fallen to the floor with a clean one, (**c**) remind guests to use clean plates for each trip to the salad bar, (**d**) wash your hands often while serving.

18. The two categories of computer hardware in the restaurant are (**a**) visual and nonvisual, (**b**) terminal and enter (**c**) back office and dining area, (**d**) electrical and battery-operated.

19. The server terminals in the dining room are activated by the server's (**a**) code number, (**b**) identity key, (**c**) authorizing card, (**d**) code number, identity key, or authorizing card.

20. When using a computer, validate each check total as proof of settlement by (**a**) having the headwaiter sign it, (**b**) inserting the guest check back into the terminal, (**c**) stamping it with the restaurant approval seal, (**d**) having the guest sign it.

21. Restaurants managers use computers to (**a**) improve their serving system, (**b**) improve their decor; (**c**) improve advertisement feedback, (**d**) replace the servers.

22. Fill the wine glasses (**a**) 1/4 to 1/3 full, (**b**) 1/3 to 1/2 full, (**c**) 1/2 to 2/3 full, (**d**) to the rim.

23. A cloth napkin is wrapped around the bottle of sparkling wine when opening it to (**a**) maintain the wine's temperature and protect your hands, (**b**) hide the label from view, (**c**) keep your hands from getting cold, (**d**) protect the wine from the light.

24. A liquor distilled from wine or a fermented fruit mash is (**a**) gin, (**b**) whiskey, (**c**) rum, (**d**) brandy.

25. An example of an afterdinner drink is a (**a**) whiskey sour, (**b**) Manhattan, (**c**) dry sherry, (**d**) crème de menthe.

GLOSSARY

A

A la (ah-lah) Prepared in a particular manner

A la carte (ah-lah-CART) Foods prepared to order; each dish separately priced

A la king Food served in a white sauce with mushrooms, green peppers, and pimientos

A la mode (ah-lah-MOHD) Usually dessert with ice cream; sometimes style of the day

Alfresco dining (al-FRES-ko) Serving food in the fresh air; outdoors

Allemande (al-mângd) Wine sauce with butter, egg yolk, and catsup that gives it a yellow color when combined

Amandine (ah-mahn-DEEN) With almonds added

Ambrosia (am-BROH-zha) Fruit dessert consisting of oranges, bananas, and shredded coconut

Americano Espresso diluted with steaming water; a weaker espresso

Anglaise (ng-glayz) Cooked in water or stock

Antipasto (ahn-tee-PAHS-toh) Italian appetizer that includes raw vegetables, fish, and meat

Appetizer (Ap-a-TI-zar) Drinks or assorted small, dainty snacks served before a meal to stimulate desire for food

Aspic (As-pick) Clear vegetable, meat, fish, or poultry jelly

Au gratin (ah-GRAH-tin) Prepared with a sauce and baked with a topping of bread crumbs and cheese

Au jus (oh-ZHUE) With unthickened natural juices

B

Bagel (BA-gel) A ring-shaped roll with a tough, chewy texture, made from plain yeast dough that is dropped briefly into nearly boiling water and then baked

Baked Cooked by hot, moist heat, usually in an oven

Baked Alaska Ice cream on cake, covered with meringue and baked in an oven until the meringue browns

Bardé (bar-day) Covered with pork or bacon slices

Basted Stock, drippings, or fat moistening or spooned over food while cooking

Battered Covered with a mixture of flour and liquid of a consistency that can be stirred

Bavarian or **Bavarois** (bav-ar-waz) Cream gelatin with whipped cream folded into it as it begins to become stiff

Béarnaise sauce (bair-NEZ) Sauce similar to hollandaise and containing tarragon

Béchamel (bay-shah-MEL) A rich cream or white sauce

Beef á la mode (bef-ah-lah-mod) Larded piece of beef cooked slowly in water with vegetables; similar to braised beef

Beef Stroganoff Sautéed tenderloin of beef with a sour cream sauce

Belevue (bel-vu) Food enclosed in aspic that can be seen

Benedictine (bay-nay-dik-tang) Liqueur made in Europe

Beurre noir (burr-NWAHR) Butter cooked to a dark brown, to which capers and a dash of vinegar are added

Biscotte (bis-kot) Biscuit or rusk

Bisque (bisk) Rich cream soup often made with seafood

Blanquette (blang-ket) White stew often made with veal

Blinis Russian buckwheat pancakes often served with caviar

Blue cheese Similar to Roquefort in appearance but made of cow's milk instead of sheep's milk

Boeuf (buhf) Beef

Bombe (bongh) or **Bombe glace** Frozen dessert that is a combination of two or more frozen mixtures packed in a round mold

Bonne femme (bong Bun) Simple home-style soups, stews, etc.

Bordelaise (bobr-dib-LztFZ) Brown sauce made with butter or marrow fat, meat stock, bay leaf, onions, carrots, red or white wine, and seasonings

Borsch or **Borscht** (borsh or borsht) Russian or Polish soup made with beets

Bouillabaisse (boo-yah-BAYS) Several varieties of fish fixed as a stew

Bouillon (BULL-yon) Meat broth

Bourgeois (boo-zhwaz) Often means served with vegetables

Braised Meats or vegetables browned in small amount of fat and then cooked covered

Breaded Rolled in bread crumbs or other breading agent before cooking

Brioche (bre-yosh) A lightly sweetened rich bread

Broche (brosh) Skewer or spit for roasting

Brochette (broh-SHET) Meat broiled on a skewer

Brunoise (brun-wahz) Finely diced

Buffet Assorted hot and cold foods displayed and ready to eat; usually self service from heated and cooled counter

 C

Cacciatore (caht-chah-TOH-rih) Sauce containing tomatoes, onions, garlic, and herb spices; wine may be added

Caesar salad (SEE-zer) Green salad with anchovies, croutons, Parmesan cheese, coddled eggs, and garlic

Café (kaf-ay) Coffee, coffee house, or restaurant

Canadian bacon Smoked loin of trimmed, lean pork

Canapé (kan-a-PAY) Spicy food mixture spread on crackers, toast, or bread

Cannelloni (Kan-a-lo-ne) Pasta or crêpe stuffed with cheese or meat and served with tomato or meat sauce

Capon (kah-POHN) Castrated poultry noted for tenderness and flavor

Cappuccino (CA-pa-CHE-no) Equal parts of brewed espresso, steamed milk, froth from the steamed milk, and often served with sugar

Carte du jour (kar-du-zhoor) Menu of the day

Casaba Large, oval melon with yellow skin and white meat

Caviar (ka-vee-ARE) Grey and black eggs or roe of fish; red eggs if from salmon

Cepes (sep) A particular species of mushroom

Champignons (shahm-pee-nyohn) Mushrooms

Chanterelles (shahn-tee-rels) Species of mushrooms

Chantilly cream (shahn-tee-YEE) Vanilla whipped cream

Chantilly sauce (shahn-tee-YEE) Hollandaise sauce with whipped cream

Chartreuse (shar-truhz) A food with a hidden filling; also a certain liqueur

Châteaubriand (shah-toh-bree-AHN) Thick tenderloin steak

Chaud (shô) Hot

Chef Person in charge of food preparation

Chef's salad Green salad topped with strips of ham, cheese, and chicken

Chemise (sh-mez) or **En chemise** Skins on; often refers to potatoes

Chiffonade (sher-fon-ad) Shredded vegetables sprinkled on salads or soups

Cloche (klosh) Dish cover

Club sandwich Sandwich made with three layers of bread or toast, and filled with chicken, bacon, and tomato

Cobbler Deep-dish fruit pie or drink of wine or liquor, sugar, sliced fruit, and mint

Cocktail An appetizer or an alcoholic drink

Compote (KOM-pote) Stewed fruit combination

Confit or **Confiture** (kon-fee) Fruit jam or preserves

Consommé (kon-so-MAY) Clear broth

Continental breakfast Assorted juices, coffee, sweet rolls, and other food items already prepared

Course Part of a meal served at one time

Creole (KRE-ol) Made with tomatoes, onions, peppers, and seasoning

Crêpes suzette (krape-su-ZET) Thin, fried pancakes covered with a sauce of liqueur and served flaming

Croissant (krwa-sang) Crescent-shaped roll or sometimes a confectionery

Croutons (KROO-tahns) Small cubes of bread fried or baked until brown

Cuisine (kwee-ZEEN) Cookery; also kitchen

Curry East Indian type of stew made with curios powder

 D

Dejeuner (DAY-zhuh-nay) Breakfast or lunch

De la maison (de-lah-ma-zon) House specialty

Demi (de-mee) Half

Demitasse (DEM-ih-tabs) Small cup of strong coffee

Diable Deviled

Diner (de-nay) Dinner or to dine

Drawn butter Melted butter

Dry Beverage with a low percentage of sugar such as dry wine or vin sec

Duchesses potatoes Mashed with eggs and forced through pastry tube

Duglére (doog-lar) Tomatoes are used

Du jour (de ZHUER) Of the day

Dusted Sprinkled with sugar or flour

E

Ecarlate (ay-kar-lat) Red sauce made with lobster or red tongue

Éclair (ay-KLMR) Oblong cream puff filled with custard and iced

Eggplant Large, purple-skinned, pear-shaped vegetable

Eggs Benedict (bay-nay-DICK) Poached egg served with ham or tongue with hollandaise sauce on toasted muffin

Emincé (ay-man-SzY) Cut finely

En casserole (abn-kads-ROL) Food served in the dish it was baked in; also fireproof dish with cover

Enchilada Mexican dish consisting of meat or cheese rolled in a tortilla covered with a peppery tomato sauce

En coquille (abn-kob-KEE) In the shell, such as oysters on the half shell

Entrée (ON-stay) Main course of a meal

Escargot (es-kar-GO) Snail

Espagnole (ays-pab-nyol) Brown sauce

Espresso (es-PRES-o) A very strong black coffee made of coffe beans roasted black and brewed under steam pressure in an espresso machine

Ethnic-fusion dishes A menu item in which ingredients from two or more ethnic cuisines

 F

Fanchonette (tang-sbo-net) Tiny pie or tart covered with meringue

Farce (Bsbes) Stuffing or forcemeat

Farci (tar-see) Stuffed

Farina Coarsely ground inner portion of hard wheat

Farinaceous Made with meal of flour

Femiére (fsir-mee-AIR) Made with diced potatoes, carrots, onions, turnips, celery, and cabbage; also farmer-style

Fettuccine Square or convex long pasta

Filet mignon (fib-LAy meen-YONE) Beef tenderloin

Fillet (fib-LAY) Boneless cut of meat or fish

Finnan haddie Smoked haddock

Flambé (fiabm-BAY) Served with flaming liqueur

Flenron (fiurr-obn) Baked, crescent-shaped puff paste used as a garnish often for fish or white sauce

Florentine (fioor-abn-teen) With spinach

Foie gras (Uwa-gra) Fat liver; most often liver of fat geese

Fondue (tong-dil) Melted or blended

Forcemeat Chopped meat with seasoning used for stuffing

Franconia Browned; usually potatoes browned with a roast

Frappé (frap-pay) Beaten and iced drink

Fromage (frob-MAHZH) Cheese

 G

Garbanzo (gar-ban4bo) Chickpea

Garnish or **Garniture** (gar-nee-tur) Decorate; food item used to decorate

Gefilte fish Fish dumpling

Gherkins Pickled, small, young cucumbers

Giblets Poultry liver heart, and trimmings

Glacé (glab-say) Glossy or semitransparent coating

Gnocchi Italian dumpling

Gourmet (goor-may) Expert connoisseur of food and drinks

Gratin or **Gratinée** (grab-tan) Dusted or sprinkled with cheese or buttered crumbs and baked brown

Gruyère (grae-YNl1x) Swiss cheese that tastes tarter and has smaller boles than regular Swiss cheese

Guava Apple- or pear-shaped tropical fruit with an acidic, sweet flavor made into jams and jellies

Gumbo Soup often made of seafood or chicken, okra, green peppers, and tomatoes

 H

Haché (bab-sbay) Chopped or minced

Hasenpfeffer Rabbit stew

Hollandaise (aw4awn-DEZ) Sauce made with egg yolk, butter and lemon juice

Hors d'oeuvres (or-DURV) Small appetizers

Hush puppies Southern deep-fried cornmeal cakes

 I

Indian pudding Slowly baked dessert made of cornmeal, milk, brown sugar eggs, and raisins

Italienne (e-tiil-yang) Italian-style

J

Jardiniere tybar-dee-MAm) With vegetables
Johnnycake Cornbread made from yellow cornmeal, eggs, and milk
Julienne (joo-ilb-EN) Thin strips of food
Jus (zhue) Juices from meat

K

Kabob (ka-BOB) Cubes of meat and other foods cooked on a skewer
Kipper Method of preserving herring, salmon, and other fish
Kosher foods Biblical term used to describe foods that are permitted to be eaten by people of the Jewish faith. Some feel they represent quality, cleanliness, and purity
Kosher-style Misleading and deceptive term indicating an ethnic form of cooking and not pertaining to Jewish dietary laws
Kuchen (kaB-ekben) Cake

L

Lait (lay) Milk
Laitue (lay-tIt) Lettuce
Langouste (labn-goost) Crawfish
Lasagne Frilly or curly-edged pasta
Latte (lah-TA) Coffee beverage which is predominently cream
Lebkuchen (iM-kBtt-ckben) German sweet cakes or honey cakes
Leek Small, onionlike vegetable
Legume (lay-GEWAf) Vegetable; also such foods as peas, beans, and lentils
Limpa Swedish rye bread
Linguine Square or convex long pasta
Lox Smoked salmon
Lyonnaise (LFE-a-NAYZ) Sliced or chopped food fried in butter with onions

M

Madrilene (mab-dree-LAlIN) Clear consommé with tomato seasoning served hot or jellied

Maître d'hôtel (mab-tre-dob-TEL) Head of catering department head of food service

Maître d'hôtel, à la (mal4re-dob-TEL) Yellow sauce; butter sauce with lemon juice and parsley

Manhattan clam chowder Made with tomatoes, vegetables, and quahog clams

Manicotti Pasta tubes, usually ridged

Maraschino (mab-rabs-KEE-nob) Italian cherry cordial; also cherries

Marengo Sautéed veal or chicken with tomatoes, mushrooms, olives, and olive oil

Marinade (mar-e-nad) French sauce used to tenderize meats and vegetables

Marsala Pale golden, semi-dry wine from Sicily

Matelote (mab-e-lot) Fish stewed with onions and wine; also fish stews

Medaillion or **Medallion** Small round or oval serving of food; often meat fillets

Melba toast Thin slices or oven-dried toast

Menthe, crème de (krem-de-MAHNT) Peppermint cordial

Meringue (may-rang) Paste of egg whites and sugar souffléd

Meunière (me-nee-air) Fish dipped in flour sautéed in butter and served with brown butter lemon, and parsley

Milanese (me-lan-ayz) Garnish consisting of julienne of ham, mushroom, tongue, and truffles

Minced Chopped fine

Minestrone (mee-nay-strob-nay) A macaroni product and cheese in a vegetable soup

Mixed grill Three kinds of meat broiled together and served on one plate

Mocha (MOH-ka) Coffee and chocolate mixed together

Mocktails Alcohol-free versions of popular cocktails

Mongol soup A soup made with tomatoes, split peas, and julienne vegetables

Mornay (mor-NAY) White sauce with cheese

Mortadella Italian pork and beef sausage

Mostaccioli Round, hollow pasta that is smooth or ribbed

Mousse (moose) Chilled dessert of whipped cream, gelatin, and flavoring

Mozzarella Soft Italian cheese

Mulligatawny A thick soup seasoned with curry

Mushroom sauce Sauce made with fat, flour stock, sliced mushrooms, seasoning, and wine

N

Napoleons Layered oblong pastry with custard, cream, or jam filling

Neapolitan Dessert of No to four kinds of ice cream, ice, or gelatin of different colors

Neat (net) Liquor taken in shot glasses without ice mixes

Nesselrode pudding Frozen dessert made with custard, chestnuts, fruit, and cream

Newburg Creamed dish made with seafood and egg yolk and flavored with sherry

Normande (nor-mand) A smooth, delicate mixture containing whipped cream

 O

Okra Vegetable pods often used in soups and gumbos

Omelet or **Omelette** Beaten egg mixture that is cooked and filled with foods such as cheese or meat

Oysters, bluepoints Oysters from the Atlantic Coast

P

Panache (pah-NASH) Mixture of several kinds of birds, fruits, and vegetables with contrasting colors

Pané (pan-ay) Breaded

Papaya A tropical fruit

Parboiled Boiled until partially cooked

Parfait (par-FAY) Ice cream, fruit, and whipped cream in tall, slender stemmed glasses

Parisienne potatoes Made with a small round scoop; can be browned, steamed, or boiled

Parmesan Grated, hard, sharp cheese used for toppings, soup, and soufflés

Parve or **Pareve** (PAR-ve) Jewish class of food which is neither meat nor dairy and includes products like grains, vegetables, vegetable oils, shortenings, and seasonings

Pastrami (pa-STRA-mi) Beef cured with spices

Paysanne (pay-sabn) Vegetables cut into square shapes

Petit (pub-tee) Small

Petite dejeuner (pub-TEE-day-zbub-HAY) Breakfast

Petite marmite (pub4eet-mabr-MEET) Consommé with chicken, beef, and vegetables; also an earthenware pot Petits fours (pab4ee-FOOR) Small cakes and cookies usually served with desserts

Petits fours (pah-tee-FOOR) Small cakes and cookies usually served with desserts

Pièce de résistance (pee-es-de-nsy-zee-STuINS) Main dish

Pilaf or **Pilaú** (pee-LOll) Sautéed rice with onions and stock; also with meats and vegetables

Piquant (pee-KAHN) or (pee-kabnt) Highly seasoned Poached Cooked in water with light bubbles or simmering at 205~ Poisson (pwab-sobn) Fish

Poached Cooked in water with light bubbles or simmering at 205°F

Poisson (pwah-sohn) Fish

Polanise (pob-ob-nayz) Garnish of bread crumbs browned in butter chopped hard-cooked egg, beurre noir and chopped parsley

Pommes de terr (pom-de-tair) Potatoes

Popovers Quick, individual, puffed-up butter rolls made of milk, flour and eggs

Postum Coffee substitute made of cereal

Potage (po-'lAHZH) Soup

Pot-au-feu (pot-ob-FE) Boiled meats and assorted vegetables with meat broth

Potpourri (pob-poo-illEE) Mixture

Poulet (poo-lay) Chicken

Prosciutto Dry-cured, spiced ham

Purée (pu-ray) Paste or pulp of fruit or vegetable; also thick soup

■■■Q

Quahog (kaub-baug) Round clams from Atlantic Coast

Quenelles (kay-NEL) Dumplings

Quiche Combination of cream, eggs, swiss cheese, and other ingredients baked in a prebaked pie shell

■■■R

Ragout (rab-GOO) Thick stew

Ramekin Individual portion of some food baked in a halting dish, often topped with cheese and bread crumbs; also small baking dish Rigatoni Cylindrical pasta, either smooth or ribbed

Rigatoni Cylindrical pasta, either smooth or ribbed

Rissole Browned; also a small turnover

Rissole potatoes or **Pommes risolees** Potatoes cut into egg shapes, browned, and finished in an oven

Riz (ree) Rice

Romaine (ro-MAIN) Narrow long, crisp-leaved lettuce with light-colored inner leaves

Roquefort cheese (ROKE-furt) Semi-hard, white cheese speckled with mold and made only in Roquefort, France

Roulade Rolled thin piece of meat, with or without stuffing, that is braised or sautéed

Russian dressing A salad dressing of mayonnaise, lemon juice, chili sauce, Worcestershire sauce, and pimiento

 S

Sanitize (SAN-i-tiz) Effective bactericidal treatment to clean surfaces of equipment, utensils, etc.; disinfect

Sautéed Cooked quickly in a small amount of fat

Schaum torte (scboum tot4e) Foam cake made of meringue and crushed fruit Serviette Table napkin Shad A type of herring Shallot A type of onion Shirred eggs Eggs baked in a shallow dish

Serviette Table napkin

Shad A type of herring

Shallot A type of onion

Shirred eggs Eggs baked in a shallow dish

Shoestring potatoes Potatoes cut very thin and french-fried

Simmered Slowly cooked just below boiling point at 205°F

Skewered Meat, poultry or vegetables fastened on long pin during cooking

Smorgasbord (smur-gaes-board) A buffet featuring a large selection of food

Sole Flat, whitefish

Sommelier (sob-meb-DilAY) Wine steward

Soufflé (soo-FLAY) Baked dish made from beaten egg whites combined with egg yolks and various other ingredients, such as cheese, spinach, chicken, or chocolate

Spinach lasagne or **noodles** Lasagne or noodles that are green because of their spinach content

Sports bar A bar where alcoholic beverages and food are served and large televisions feature sports events

Stir-fry (STER-fri) To stir very fast while frying in a little oil or fat

 T

Tableware All multiuse eating and drinking utensils, including knives, forks, and spoons

Tartar sauce A sauce for seafood made of mayonnaise and pickle relish

Timbales Little pastry shell filled with mixture of chicken, seafood, cheese, fish, or vegetables

Tortiglioni Cylindrical pasta that can be smooth or ribbed Tortillas Mexican corn pancakes

Tortillas Mexican corn pancakes

Tournedos (toor-nub-DOE) Small tenderloin steaks Tripe Inner lining of beef stomachs

Tripe Inner lining of beef stomachs

Truffles Mushroomlike fungus grown underground

Tutti-frutti (TOO4ee-froo-tee) Fruit mixture, as in ice cream

 V

Veal birds Veal sliced thin, rolled around stuffing, and then stewed or cooked in covered casserole

Veloute (vel-oot-eb) A cream soup or a thick, creamy sauce Vermicelli Thin spaghetti

Vermicelli Thin spaghetti

Vichyssoise (vee-sbee-SWAZ) Cold potato and leek soup Vinaigrette (vee-neb-GRET) Dressing made with oil, vinegar; and herbs Waldorf salad Apples, celery, nuts, and mayonnaise

Vinaigrette (vee-neh-GRET) Dressing made with oil, vinegar, and herbs

W

Waldorf salad Apples, celery, nuts, and mayonnaise

Watercress Crisp, green leaves of a plant in the mustard family that is used in salads, sandwiches, and garnishes

Wiener schnitzel (Vee-ner-SCHNIT-zl) Breaded veal cutlet served with lemon

Wild rice Not a true rice but the seeds of a northern water grass; often served with game

Wonton Noodle dough stuffed with ground chicken or pork and often added to Chinese soups

 Y

Yam Tuber similar to sweet potato

Yorkshire pudding Baked egg and flour mixture served with roast beef

Zucchini (zoo-KE-nE) Italian summer squash

Adams, Leon D. *The Commonsense Book of Wine*. New York: McGraw-Hill Book Company, 1986.

_____. *The Wines of America*. 4th ed. New York: McGraw-Hill Publishing Company, 1990.

Aidells, Bruce, and Kelly, Dennis. *Real Beer & Good Eats: The Rebirth of America's Beer and Food Traditions*. New York: Alfred A. Knopf, Inc., 1992

Alert Cab: An Action Program to Reduce the Incidence of Drunk Driving. St Louis: Anheuser-Busch, Inc., 1990.

Anderson, Will. *The Beer Book*. Philadelphia: The Pyne Press, 1973.

Bespaloff, Alexis. *Alexis Bespaloff's Complete Guide to Wine*. New York: Penguin Books, 1994.

Berger, Dan. "Restaurant Wine Protocol Varies, But Here's Some Advice." *Minneapolis Star Tribune*, Feb. 22, 1995, Taste section, p. 41.

Blue, Anthony Dias. *American wine: A comprehensive guide*. New York: Doubleday & Company, 1985.

Briefing. *The Restaurateurs News Digest* October 1985, vol. 9, no. 10.

Broadbent, Michael. *The Complete Guide to Wine Tasting and Wine Cellars*. New York: Simon and Schuster, 1984.

Cooper, Roselind. *Spirits & Liqueurs*. Tucson: HP Books, 1982.

"Focus on Computerized Cash Control." *Nation's Restaurant News*, July 2, 1984, sec. 2, pp. 17–19.

Foodservice Editors of CBI. *The Professional Host*. New York: Van Nostrand Reinhold, 1981.

Godsey, Kristin Dunlap. "Fire in the Kitchen." *R & I Action Plan*, February 15, 1995, pp. 88–94.

Hartmann, Thomas. "How Computer Control Tamed the Confusion of Success." *List*, March, 1984.

Hellmich, Nanci. "Sharing Tips for Both Waiters and Diners." *USA Today*, June 22, 1994, Life section.

Herbst, Ron, and Herbst, Sharon Tyler. *Wine Lover's Companion*. New York: Barrons Publishing Co., 1995.

Indiana State Department of Health. *What is Hepatitis A?* Fact Sheet, 1993.

Jackson, Michael. ed. *Michael Jackson's Beer Companion*. Philadelphia: Running Press Book Publishers, 1994.

Johnson, Hugh. *Vintage: The Story of Wine*. New York: Simon and Schuster, 1989.

King, Carol. *Professional Dining Room Management*. 2nd ed. New York: Van Nostrand Reinhold, 1988.

Kolpan, Steven, Smith, Brian H., and Weiss, Michael A. *Exploring Wine: The Culinary Institute of America's Guide to Wines of the World*. New York: Van Nostrand Reinhold, 1996.

Kramer, Matt. *Making Sense of Wine*. New York: William Morrow and Company, Inc., 1989.

Lipinski, Robert A., and Lipinski, Kathleen A. *Professional Guide to Alcoholic Beverages*. New York: Van Nostrand Reinhold, 1989.

Lorenzini, Beth, and Johnson, Brad A. "Restaurant Wars." *R & I The Staff*, May 1, 1995, pp. 148–157.

"Making Computers Work for You." *Nation's Restaurant News*, July 1, 1985, sec. 2.

Massee, William. *Massee's Wine Almanac*. Englewood Cliffs, NJ: Prentice-Hall, Inc., 1980.

Meyer, Sylvia, Schmid, Edy, and Spühler, Christel. *Professional Table Service*. Tran. Heinz Holtmann. New York: Van Nostrand Reinhold, 1990.

Minnesota Restaurant Association. *Smoking in Restaurants and Bars*. Minneapolis: MRA Division of Environmental Health, 1994.

Mira. Linda. *Guide to Good Service*. Lake Worth: Florida Printing Company, 1986.

National Restaurant Association. "High-Tech Hospitality: 1995 Food Service Industry Forecast." *Restaurants USA*, December, 1994, vol. 14, no. 11, pp. 15–38.

National Restaurant Association. "Liquor Liability and the Restaurant Industry." *Current Issues Report*, 1984–1985.

NCR Corporation. *NCR 2160 Bar/Restaurant Control System*, 1985.

O'Neal, Jon T. *OSHA Bloodborne Pathogen Standard, A Pragmatic Approach*. New York: Van Nostrand Reinhold, (Forthcoming, 1996).

Pogash, Jeffery. *How to Read a Wine Label*. New York: Hawthorn Books, Inc., 1978.

Regan, Gary. *The Bartender's Bible*. New York: Harper Collins Publishers, 1991.

Remanco Systems. *Management Course Book*.

Riell, Howard. "Wine Sales á la Card." *Cheers*, April, 1995, pp. 55–60.

Riely, Elizabeth. *The Chef's Companion: A Concise Dictionary of Culinary Terms*. New York: Van Nostrand Reinhold, 1986.

Robinson, Jancis. *The Oxford Companion to Wine*. New York: Oxford University Press, 1994.

Rubash, Joyce. *Master Dictionary of Food & Wine*. New York: Van Nostrand Reinhold, 1990.

Scroggin, Daniel R. " 'Happy Hour' in Sober Spot." *Nation's Restaurant News*, November 4, 1985, vol. 19, p. F13.

Seaberg, Albin. *Menu Design: Merchandising and Marketing*. 4th ed. New York: Van Nostrand Reinhold, 1991.

Sennett, Bob. *Complete World Bartenders Guide*. New York: Bantam Books, 1993.

Shugart, Grace, and Molt, Mary. *Food for Fifty*. New York: John Wiley & Sons, 1993.

Smith, Gregg. *The Beer Enthusiasts Guide*. Pownal, VT: BookCrafters, 1994.

Sonnenschmidt, Frederic H. and Nicolas, John. *The Professional Chef's Art of Garde Manger* 5th ed. New York: Van Nostrand Reinhold, 1993.

Spence, Molly. "Emergency." *R & I Action Plan*, May 15, 1995, pp. 144–150.

Spurrier, Steven and Dovaz, Michel. *Academie du Vin Complete Wine Course*. New York: G. P Putnam's Sons, 1983.

Thompson, Bob. *Guide to California's Wine Country*. Menlo Park, CA: Lane Publishing Co., 1982.

United States Public Health Service. *Food Code 1993*. Washington, DC.

Walker, Michael. *The Cocktail Book*. London: London Editions Limited, 1980.

Walton, J. Banch. "Dealing with Dangerous Employees." *Security Management Magazine*, September, 1993, pp. 9–10.

"Welcome to the Wonderful World of Kosher Cuisine." Handout for New York Restaurant and Foodservice Show. Kosher Coordinators, Ltd.

Zraly, Kevin. *Windows on the World Complete Wine Course*. New York: Sterling Publishing Co., 1985.

ART CREDITS

CHAPTER 1

Figure 1–1   Courtesy of Crest Uniform Company, Inc.

CHAPTER 2

Figure 2–1   Courtesy of The Culinary Institute of America

Figure 2–3   Courtesy of Johnson & Wales University

Figure 2–8   Courtesy of Johnson & Wales University

Figure 2–9   Hometown Buffet, Inc.

Figure 2–10   Courtesy Culinary Architect Catering, New York City and Port Washington, New York. Photo by Alexandra Troy.

Figure 2–11   Courtesy of The New York Restaurant Group, Inc.

CHAPTER 3

Figure 3–1   Hartsville Country Club (Steve Roos, photographer)

Figure 3–2a–e   Courtesy of Johnson & Wales University

Figure 3–3   Lakeside Manufacturing, Inc.

Figure 3–4   Key West Shrimp House, Madison, Indiana

Figure 3–5   Courtesy of Amana Refrigeration, Inc. Information on Kosher foods provided by Kosher Coordinators, Ltd. Your Bridge to the World of Kosher Events, 1452 Beacon Place, Bayswater, New York 11691-1608

CHAPTER 4

Figure 4–1   Courtesy of Johnson & Wales University

Figure 4–2   Courtesy of The Four Seasons Restaurant

Figure 4–7   The Abbey (Wally E. Schulz, photographer)

Figure 4–8   Kurt Kahl, photographer

Figure 4–10   Key West Shrimp House (Jim Pirtle, photographer)

CHAPTER 5

Figure 5–1   © The Photo Works/courtesy Bryant Park Grill, New York City

Figure 5–2   Courtesy of Johnson & Wales University

Figure 5–3 © The Photo Works/courtesy Gemini Restaurant, New York City

Figure 5–4 Courtesy of Hyatt Hotels & Resorts (David Kryszak, photographer)

Figure 5–5 Courtesy of Johnson & Wales University

Figure 5–6 Courtesy of First Bank-Minneapolis, Minneapolis, Minnesota

Figure 5–7a Courtesy of American Express Company, Citibank, Discover Card Services, Inc., MasterCard, TransMedia Service Company, Inc., and Visa

Figure 5–7c Courtesy of American Express Company and DesignLin Advertising, Ltd.

Figure 5–8 The Abbey (Wally E. Schulz, photographer)

▉▉▉ CHAPTER 6

Figure 6–1 © The Photo Works/courtesy Gemini Restaurant, New York City

Figure 6–2 © The Photo Works/courtesy Bryant Park Grill, New York City

Figure 6–3 Courtesy HumanCentric Solutions Inc.

Figure 6–5 Courtesy New York City Department of Health, the City of New York

▉▉▉ CHAPTER 7

Figure 7–1 Courtesy of Polytel Computer Products Corp.

Figure 7–2 NCR Corporation

Figure 7–3 Courtesy of MicroTouch Systems, Inc.

Figure 7–4 Courtesy of Polytel Computer Products Corp.

Figure 7–5 Courtesy of Telequip Corporation

Figure 7–6 Courtesy Panasonic Communications & Systems Company, POS Systems Division

Figure 7–7 Micros Systems, Inc.

Figure 7–8 Courtesy of AT&T Global Information Systems

Figure 7–9 Micros Systems, Inc.

Figure 7–10 Courtesy of Omron Systems, Inc.

Figure 7–11 Courtesy of Rapidfire Software, Inc.

Figure 7–12 Ogle Haus Inn (Jim Pirtle, photographer)

▉▉▉ CHAPTER 8

Table 8–1 Reprinted with the permission of the National Restaurant Association

Figure 8–1 Courtesy of National Restaurant Association

Figure 8–2 Courtesy of Robert Mondavi Winery

Figure 8–4 Courtesy of The Four Seasons Restaurant

Index